True Irish
Ghost Stories

True Irish Ghost Stories

A Collection of First-hand Tales of the Paranormal

St. John D. Seymour
and Harry L. Neligan

This edition published in 2024 by Arcturus Publishing Limited
26/27 Bickels Yard, 151–153 Bermondsey Street,
London SE1 3HA

AD011556UK

Printed in the UK

MIX
Paper | Supporting
responsible forestry
FSC® C171272

Contents

Introduction

BORN in 1880 in Limerick, Ireland, St. John Drelincourt Seymour was educated at Trinity College, Dublin and was ordained as an Anglican priest in 1904. Despite his devoutly religious nature, Seymour was deeply interested in the folklore, fairy tales and medieval stories of Ireland and the Irish people. He carried out a great deal of research on Irish folklore while working in the Church as a curate in Durrow and Thurles and the incumbent at Toem and Borris. He eventually became the Archdeacon of Cashel, Emly and Donohil but is best known for his books *Irish Witchcraft and Demonology, The Tales of King Solomon* and T*rue Irish Ghost Stories.*

This collection of ghost stories came into being as a result of Seymour noticing an informational gap in his work on witchcraft and demonology. He had just finished research for his book, *Irish Witchcraft and Demonology,* when he realised there was no prominent collection of Irish ghost stories in circulation.

True Irish Ghost Stories is a collection of solicited accounts of ghostly activity witnessed by the people of Ireland as well as those gathered by Seymour himself during his time as archdeacon. These accounts were compiled by Seymour, who was assisted by Mr. Harry L. Neligan, D.I. Neligan was a British police officer and writer who helped establish the Royal Ulster Constabulary. In true mystery-writing fashion, Seymour is not particularly forthcoming about how the work was divided between himself and Neligan, and in the preface, he writes "I leave it as a pleasant task to the Higher Critic to discover what portions of the book were done by him, and what should be attributed to me."

In this book, you will experience various spooky tales such as that shared by Mrs. G. Kelly, whose home was repeatedly visited by an apparition of a large and smiling elderly woman. Her chilling experience describes the haunting of a residence which upended visiting guests as well as the organisation of the Kelly family's home. Later, you will learn about death symbols that besieged the Westropp family, like the headless coach that forewarned the death of Ralph Westropp long before the arrival of the doctor. Varied and utterly gripping, these ghost stories reflect the experiences, traditions, beliefs and histories of the Irish people.

This collection varies in origin, content and form, allowing for different stories and storytelling styles to be highlighted. Haunted houses, poltergeists, apparitions, banshees, ancestral ghosts and mistaken identities are but a few of the subjects unleashed on the coming pages. Seymour and Neligan give the frightful accounts witnessed by ordinary citizens of Ireland not only profound deference and experiential recognition, but literary significance as well. The first publication's popularity prompted a second expanded edition complete with more accounts of ghosts and the supernatural, with particular emphasis on haunted houses. It is this version that is included here. Notably popular in the English press, the poltergeist accounts were specifically considered to be too similar to traditional Irish folktales whereas the invisible ghosts and haunted house stories were received with less scepticism.

On the factual nature of these stories, Seymour says, "For myself I cannot guarantee the genuineness of a single incident in this book—how could I, as none of them are my own personal experience? This at least I *can* vouch for, that the majority of the stories were sent to me as first or second-hand experiences by ladies and gentlemen whose statement on an ordinary matter of fact would be accepted without question." It is therefore due to Seymour's loving care and deep respect that this compilation remains cherished and relevant today. After a life of service to the Anglican church, he died in 1950 aged 70.

TO THREE LIVELY POLTERGEISTS

W—, J—, AND G—,

THIS BOOK IS DEDICATED BY THE COMPILERS

Preface to First Edition

THIS book had its origin on this wise. In my *Irish Witchcraft and Demonology* published in October 1913, I inserted a couple of famous 17th century ghost stories which described how lawsuits were set on foot at the instigation of most importunate spirits. It then occurred to me that as far as I knew there was no such thing in existence as a book of Irish ghost stories. Books on Irish fairy- and folk-lore there were in abundance—some of which could easily be spared—but there was no book of ghosts. And so I determined to supply this sad omission.

In accordance with the immortal recipe for making hare-soup I had first to obtain my ghost stories. Where was I to get them from? For myself I knew none worth publishing, nor had I ever had any strange experiences, while I feared that my friends and acquaintances were in much the same predicament. Suddenly a brilliant thought struck me. I wrote out a letter, stating exactly what I wanted, and what I did not want, and requesting the readers of it either to forward me ghost stories, or else to put me in the way of getting them: this letter was sent to the principal Irish newspapers on October 27, and published on October 29, and following days.

I confess I was a little doubtful as to the result of my experiment, and wondered what response the people of Ireland would make to a letter which might place a considerable amount of trouble on their shoulders. My mind was speedily set at rest. On October 30, the first answers reached me. Within a fortnight I had sufficient material to make a book; within a month I had so much material that I could pick and choose—and more was promised. Further on in this preface I give a list of those persons whose contributions I have made use of, but here I should like to take the opportunity of thanking all those ladies and gentlemen throughout the length and breadth of Ireland, the majority of whom were utter strangers to me, who went to the trouble of sitting down and writing out page after page of stories. I cannot forget their kindness, and I am only sorry that I could not make use of more of the matter that was sent to me. As one would expect, this material varied in value and extent. Some persons contributed incidents, of little use by themselves, but which worked in as helpful illustrations, while others forwarded budgets of stories, long and short. To sift the mass of matter, and bring the various portions of it into proper sequence, would have been a lengthy and difficult piece of work had I not been ably assisted by Mr. Harry L. Neligan, D.I.; but I leave it as a pleasant task to the Higher Critic to discover what portions of the book were done by him, and what should be attributed to me.

Some of the replies that reached me were sufficiently amusing. One gentleman, who carefully signed himself "Esquire," informed me that he was "after" reading a great book of ghost stories, but several letters of mine failed to elicit any subsequent information. Another person offered to *sell* me ghost stories, while several proffered tales that had been worked up comically. One lady addressed a card to me as follows:

"THE REV^D.——

(Name and address lost of the clergyman whose letter appeared lately in *Irish Times*, *re* "apparitions")

CAPPAWHITE."

As the number of clergy in the above village who deal in ghost stories is strictly limited, the Post Office succeeded in delivering it safely. I wrote at once in reply, and got a story. In a letter bearing the Dublin postmark a correspondent, veiled in anonymity, sent me a religious tract with the curt note, "*Re* ghost stories, will you please read this." I did so, but still fail to see the sender's point of view. Another person in a neighbouring parish declared that if I were their rector they would forthwith leave my church, and attend service elsewhere. There are many, I fear, who adopt this attitude; but it will soon become out of date.

Some of my readers may cavil at the expression "*True* Ghost Stories." For myself I cannot guarantee the genuineness of a single incident in this book—how could I, as none of them are my own personal experience? This at least I *can* vouch for, that the majority of the stories were sent to me as first- or second-hand experiences by ladies and gentlemen whose statement on an ordinary matter of fact would be accepted without question. And further, in order to prove the *bona fides* of this book, I make the following offer. The original letters and documents are in my custody at Donohil Rectory, and I am perfectly willing to allow any responsible person to examine them, subject to certain restrictions, these latter obviously being that names of people and places must not be divulged, for I regret to say that in very many instances my correspondents have laid this burden upon me. This is to be the more regretted, because the use of blanks, or fictitious initials, makes a story appear much less convincing than if real names had been employed.

Just one word. I can imagine some of my readers (to be numbered by the thousand, I hope) saying to themselves: "Oh! Mr. Seymour has left out some of the best stories. Did he never hear of such-and-such a haunted house, or place?" Or, "I could relate an experience better than anything he has got." If such there be, may I beg of them to send me on their stories with all imagined speed, as they may be turned to account at some future date.

I beg to return thanks to the following for permission to make use of matter in their publications: Messrs. Sealy, Bryers, and Walker, proprietors of the *New Ireland Review*; the editor of the *Review of Reviews*; the editor of the *Proceedings* of the Society for Psychical Research; the editor of the *Journal* of the American S.P.R.; the editor of the *Occult Review*, and Mr. Elliott O'Donnell; Messrs. Longmans, Green and Co., and Mrs. Andrew Lang; the editor of the *Wide World Magazine*; the representatives of the late Rev. Dr. Craig.

In accordance with the promise made in my letter, I have now much pleasure in giving the names of the ladies and gentlemen who have contributed to, or assisted in, the compilation of this book, and as well to assure them that Mr. Neligan and I are deeply grateful to them for their kindness.

Mrs. S. Acheson, Drumsna, Co. Roscommon; Mrs. M. Archibald, Cliftonville Road, Belfast; J. J. Burke, Esq., U.D.C., Rahoon, Galway; Capt. R. Beamish, Passage West, Co. Cork; Mrs. A. Bayly, Woodenbridge, Co. Wicklow; R. Blair, Esq., South Shields; Jas. Byrne, Esq., Castletownroche, Co. Cork; Mrs. Kearney Brooks, Killarney; H. Buchanan, Esq., Inishannon, Co. Cork; J. A. Barlow, Esq., Bray, Co. Wicklow; J. Carton, Esq., King's Inns Library, Dublin; Miss A. Cooke, Cappagh House, Co. Limerick; J. P. V. Campbell, Esq., solicitor, Dublin; Rev. E. G. S. Crosthwait, M.A., Littleton, Thurles: J. Crowley, Esq., Munster and Leinster Bank,

Cashel; Miss C. M. Doyle, Ashfield Road, Dublin; J. Ralph Dagg, Esq., Baltinglass; Gerald A. Dillon, Esq., Wicklow; Matthias and Miss Nan Fitzgerald, Cappagh House, Co. Limerick; Lord Walter Fitzgerald, Kilkea Castle; Miss Finch, Rushbrook, Co. Cork; Rev. H. R. B. Gillespie, M.A., Aghacon Rectory, Roscrea; Miss Grene, Grene Park, Co. Tipperary; L. H. Grubb, Esq., J.P., D.L., Ardmayle, Co. Tipperary; H. Keble Gelston, Esq., Letterkenny; Ven. J. A. Haydn, LL.D., Archdeacon of Limerick; Miss Dorothy Hamilton, Portarlington; Richard Hogan, Esq., Bowman St., Limerick; Mrs. G. Kelly, Rathgar, Dublin; Miss Keefe, Carnahallia, Doon; Rev. D. B. Knox, Whitehead, Belfast; Rev. J. D. Kidd, M.A., Castlewellan; E. B. de Lacy, Esq., Marlboro' Road, Dublin; Miss K. Lloyd, Shinrone, King's Co.; Canon Lett, M.A., Aghaderg Rectory; T. MacFadden, Esq., Carrigart, Co. Donegal; Wm. Mackey, Esq., Strabane; Canon Courtenay Moore, M.A., Mitchelstown, Co. Cork; J. McCrossan, Esq., journalist; Strabane; G. H. Miller, Esq., J.P., Edgeworthstown; Mrs. P. C. F. Magee, Dublin; Rev. R. D. Paterson, B.A., Ardmore Rectory; E. A. Phelps, Esq., Trinity College Library; Mrs. Pratt, Munster and Leinster Bank, Rathkeale; Miss Pirn, Monkstown, Co. Dublin; Miss B. Parker, Passage West, Co. Cork; Henry Reay, Esq., Harold's Cross, Dublin; M. J. Ryan, Esq., Taghmon, Co. Wexford; P. Ryan, Esq., Nicker, Pallasgrean; Canon Ross-Lewin, Kilmurry, Limerick; Miss A. Russell, Elgin Road, Dublin; Lt. Col. the Hon. F. Shore, Thomastown, Co. Kilkenny; Mrs. Seymour, Donohil Rectory; Mrs. E. L. Stritch, North Great Georges St., Dublin; M. C. R. Stritch, Esq., Belturbet; Very Rev. the Dean of St. Patrick's. D.D.; Mrs. Spratt, Thurles; W. S. Thompson, Esq., Inishannon, Co. Cork; Mrs, Thomas, Sandycove, Dublin; Mrs. Walker, Glenbeigh, Co. Kerry; Miss Wolfe, Skibbereen, Co. Cork; Mrs. E. Welsh, Nenagh; T.J. Westropp, Esq., M.A., M.R.I.A., Sandymount, Dublin; Mrs. M.

A. Wilkins, Rathgar, Dublin; John Ward, Esq., Ballymote; Mrs. Wrench, Ballybrack, Co. Dublin; Miss K. E. Younge, Upper Oldtown, Rathdowney.

ST. JOHN D. SEYMOUR.

DONOHIL RECTORY,
    CAPPAWHITE, TIPPERARY,
        February 2, 1914.

Preface to Second Edition

THIS book made its first appearance in December 1914. It was very well received by the reading public, and the entire edition was speedily sold out, but the disturbed state of affairs at home and abroad did not encourage the issue of a second edition. However, last July my publishers, Messrs. Hodges, Figgis, approached me on this matter, and I agreed to see what could be done about it. As before, I sent letters to the daily papers, asking for authentic ghost stories, and again I received a very generous response to my appeal. Most of the stories that are now added to the book are *first-hand* experiences, which in several instances I have taken down myself from the percipients.

I must thank the following ladies and gentlemen for their kindness in furnishing me with material: Major Beamish, Passage West, Cork; Rev. Leslie G. Davis, M. A., Castle Connell Rectory, Limerick; Miss C. Dysart, Moville, Donegal; Mrs. Dix, Wellington Road, Dublin; Miss Dorothy Emerson; Miss Kathleen G. Evans, Upper Leeson St., Dublin; Miss Fleming, Monkstown, Cork; Thomas Fahey, Esq., Tinnahinch, Annacarty, Tipperary; Rev. H. R. B. Gillespie, B.D., LL.B. (formerly of Aghancon Rectory); C. Gleeson, Esq., Nenagh; Mrs. Houlihan, National Bank House, Thurles; Thomas S. Hill, Esq., Donnybrook, Dublin; Mrs. Ada Vere Hunt,

Ardmayle, Co. Tipperary; Rev. Canon Johnstone, M.A., Bansha Rectory, Tipperary; F. R. B. Kennedy, Esq., Birr; R. Coplen Langford, Esq., Kilcosgriff, Shanagolden, Limerick; Mrs. Mansell, Toronto, Canada; Mrs. A. Notter, Station Road, Belfast; Editor, *Occult Review*; Richard Pearson, Esq., Doon, Co. Limerick; F. C. Pilkington, Esq., Hume St., Dublin; M. J. Ryan, Esq., Mulmintra, Taghmon, Wexford; Mrs. Markham Rae, Dungarvan; Miss E. M. B. Seymour, Ardfinan, Cahir; Mrs. Seale, St. Luke's Rectory, S.C.R., Dublin; Editor, *Tipperary Star*; Rev. Canon J. C. Trotter, Monkstown, Dublin; Rev. R. W. Talbot, M.A., Loughrea; Rev. Canon A. B. R. Young, M.A., Bath. Some of these contributors sent me stories so long ago as 1915.

ST. JOHN D. SEYMOUR.

DONOHIL RECTORY,
CAPPAWHITE, TIPPERARY,
September 20, 1926.

I

HAUNTED HOUSES IN OR NEAR DUBLIN

O F all species of ghostly phenomena, that commonly known as "haunted houses" appeals most to the ordinary person. There is something very eerie in being shut up within the four walls of a house with a ghost. The poor human being is placed at such a disadvantage. If we know that a gateway, or road, or field has the reputation of being haunted, we can in nearly every case make a detour, and so avoid the unpleasant locality. But the presence of a ghost in a house creates a very different state of affairs. It appears and disappears at its own sweet will, with a total disregard for our feelings: it seems to be as much part and parcel of the domicile as the staircase or the hall door, and, consequently, nothing short of leaving the house or of pulling it down (both of these solutions are not always practicable) will free us absolutely from the unwelcome presence.

There is also something so natural, and at the same time so unnatural, in seeing a door open when we know that no human hand rests on the knob, or in hearing the sound of footsteps, light or heavy, and feeling that it cannot be attributed to the feet of mortal man or woman. Or perhaps a form appears in a room, standing, sitting, or walking—in fact, situated in its three dimensions apparently as an ordinary being of flesh and blood, until it proves its unearthly nature by vanishing before our astonished eyes. Or perhaps we are asleep in bed. The room is shrouded in darkness, and our recumbent attitude, together with the weight of bed-clothes, hampers our movements and probably makes us more cowardly. A man will meet pain or danger boldly if he be standing upright—occupying that erect position which is his as Lord of Creation; but his courage does not well so high if he be supine. We are awakened suddenly by the feel that some superhuman Presence is in the room. We are transfixed with terror, we cannot find either the bell-rope or the matches, while we *dare* not leap out of bed and make a rush for the door lest we should encounter we know not what. In an agony of fear, we feel it moving towards us; it approaches closer, and yet closer, to the bed, and—for what may or may not then happen we must refer our readers to the pages of this book.

But the sceptical reader will say: "This is all very well, but—there are *no* haunted houses. All these alleged strange happenings are due to a vivid imagination, or else to rats and mice." (The question of deliberate and conscious fraud may be rejected in almost every instance.) This simple solution has been put forward so often that it should infallibly have solved the problem long ago. But will such a reader explain how it is that the noise made by rats and mice can resemble slow, heavy footsteps, or else take the form of a human being seen by several persons; or how our imagination can cause doors to open and shut, or else create a conglomeration of noises which, physically, would be beyond the power of ordinary individuals to reproduce? Whatever may be the ultimate explanation, we feel that there is a great deal in the words quoted by Professor Barrett: "In spite of all reasonable scepticism, it is difficult to avoid accepting, at least provisionally, the conclusion that there are, in a certain sense, haunted houses, *i.e.* that there are houses in which similar quasi-human apparitions have occurred at different times to different inhabitants, under circumstances which exclude the hypothesis of suggestion or expectation."

We must now turn to the subject of this chapter. Mrs. G. Kelly, a lady well known in musical circles in Dublin, sends as her own personal experience the following tale of a most quiet haunting, in which the spectral charwoman (!) does not seem to have entirely laid aside all her mundane habits.

"My first encounter with a ghost occurred about twenty years ago. On that occasion I was standing in the kitchen of my house in —— Square, when a woman, whom I was afterwards to see many times, walked down the stairs into the room. Having heard the footsteps outside, I was not in the least perturbed, but turned to look who it was, and found myself looking at a tall, stout, elderly woman, wearing a bonnet and old-fashioned mantle. She had grey hair, and a benign and amiable expression. We stood gazing at each other while one could count twenty. At first I was not at all frightened, but gradually as I stood looking at her an uncomfortable feeling, increasing to terror, came over me. This caused me to retreat farther and farther back, until I had my back against the wall, and then the apparition slowly faded.

"This feeling of terror, due perhaps to the unexpectedness of her appearance, always overcame me on the subsequent occasions on which I saw her. These occasions numbered twelve or fifteen, and I have seen her in every room in the house, and at every hour of the day, during a period of about ten years. The last time she appeared was ten years ago. My husband and I had just returned from a concert at which he had been singing, and we sat for some time over supper, talking about the events of the evening. When at last I rose to leave the room, and opened the dining-room door, I found my old lady standing on the mat outside with her head bent towards the door in the attitude of listening. I called out loudly, and my husband rushed to my side. That was the last time I have seen her.

"One peculiarity of this spectral visitant was a strong objection to disorder or untidyness of any kind, or even to an alteration in the general routine of the house. For instance, she showed her disapproval of any stranger coming to sleep by turning the chairs face downwards on the floor in the room they were to occupy. I well remember one of our guests, having gone to his room one evening for something he had forgotten, remarking on coming downstairs again, 'Well, you people have an extraordinary manner of arranging your furniture! I have nearly broken my bones over one of the bedroom chairs which was turned down on the floor.' As my husband and I had restored that chair twice already to its proper position during the day, we were not much surprised at his remarks, although we did not enlighten him. The whole family have been disturbed by a peculiar knocking which occurred in various rooms in the house, frequently on the door or wall, but sometimes on the furniture, quite close to where we had been sitting. This was evidently loud enough to be heard in the next house, for our next-door neighbour once asked my husband why he selected such curious hours for hanging his pictures. Another strange and fairly frequent occurrence was the following. I had got a set of skunk furs which I fancied had an unpleasant odour, as this fur sometimes has; and at night I used to take it from my wardrobe and lay it on a chair in the drawing-room, which was next my bedroom. The first time that I did this, on going to the drawing-room I found, to my surprise, my muff in one corner and my stole in another. Not for a moment suspecting a supernatural agent, I asked my servant about it, and she assured me that she had not been in the room that morning. Whereupon I determined to test the matter, which I did by putting in the furs late at night, and taking care that I was the first to enter the room in the morning. I invariably found that they had been disturbed."

A most weird experience fell to the lot of Major Macgregor, and was contributed by him to *Real Ghost Stories*, the celebrated Christmas number of the *Review of Reviews*. He says: "In the end of 1871 I went over to Ireland to visit a relative living in a Square in the north side of Dublin. In January 1872 the husband of my relative fell ill. I sat up with him for several nights, and at last, as he seemed better, I went to bed, and directed the footman to call me if anything went wrong. I soon fell asleep, but some time after was awakened by a push on the left shoulder. I started up, and said, 'Is there anything wrong?' I got no answer, but immediately received another push. I got annoyed, and said 'Can you not speak, man! And tell me if there is anything wrong?' Still no answer, and I had a feeling I was going to get another push when I suddenly turned round and caught a human hand, warm, plump, and soft. I said, 'Who are you?' but I got no answer. I then tried to pull the person towards me, but could not do so. I then said, 'I *will* know who you are!' and having the hand tight in my right hand, with my left I felt the wrist and arm, enclosed, as it seemed to me, in a tight-fitting sleeve of some winter material with a linen cuff, but when I got to the elbow all trace of an arm ceased. I was so astounded that I let the hand go, and just then the clock struck two. Including the mistress of the house, there were five females in the establishment, and I can assert that the hand belonged to none of them. When I reported the adventure, the servants exclaimed, 'Oh, it must have been the master's old Aunt Betty, who lived for many years in the upper part of that house, and had died over fifty years before at a great age.' I afterwards heard that the room in which I felt the hand had been considered haunted, and very curious noises and peculiar incidents occurred, such as the bed-clothes torn off, &c. One lady got a slap in the face from some invisible hand, and when she lit her candle she saw as if something opaque fell or jumped off the bed. A general officer, a brother of the lady, slept there two nights, but preferred going to a hotel to remaining the third night. He never would say what he heard or saw, but always said the room was uncanny. I slept for months in the room afterwards, and was never in the least disturbed."

A truly terrifying sight was witnessed by a clergyman in a school-house a good many years ago. This cleric was curate of a Dublin parish, but resided with his parents some distance out of town in the direction of Malahide. It not infrequently happened that he had to hold meetings in the evenings, and on such occasions, as his home was so far away, and as the modern convenience of tramcars was not then known, he used to sleep in the schoolroom, a large bare room, where the meetings were held. He had made a sleeping-apartment for himself by placing a pole across one end of the room, on which he had rigged up two curtains which, when drawn together, met in the middle. One night he had been holding some meeting, and when everybody had left he locked up the empty schoolhouse, and went to bed. It was a bright moonlight night, and every object could be seen perfectly clearly. Scarcely had he got into bed when he became conscious of some invisible presence. Then he saw the curtains agitated at one end, as if hands were grasping them on the outside. In an agony of terror he watched these hands groping along outside the curtains till they reached the middle. The curtains were then drawn a little apart, and a Face peered in—an awful, evil Face, with an expression of wickedness and hate upon it which no words could describe. It looked at him for a few moments, then drew back again, and the curtains closed. The clergyman had sufficient courage left to leap out of bed and make a thorough examination of the room, but, as he expected, he found no one. He dressed himself as quickly as possible, walked home, and never again slept a night in that schoolroom.

The following tale, sent by Mr. E. B. de Lacy, contains a most extraordinary and unsatisfactory element of mystery. He says: "When I was a boy I lived in the suburbs, and used to come in every morning to school in the city. My way lay through a certain street in which stood a very dismal semi-detached house, which, I might say, was closed up regularly about every six months. I would see new tenants coming into it, and then in a few months it would be 'To let' again. This went on for eight or nine years, and I often wondered what was the reason. On inquiring one day from a friend, I was told that it had the reputation of being haunted.

"A few years later I entered business in a certain office, and one day it fell to my lot to have to call on the lady who at that particular period was the tenant of the haunted house. When we had transacted our business she informed me that she was about to leave. Knowing the reputation of the house, and being desirous of investigating a ghost-story, I asked her if she would give me the history of the house as far as she knew it, which she very kindly did as follows:

"About forty years ago the house was left by will to a gentleman named ——. He lived in it for a short time, when he suddenly went mad, and had to be put in an asylum. Upon this his agents let the house to a lady. Apparently nothing unusual happened for some time, but a few months later, as she went down one morning to a room behind the kitchen, she found the cook hanging by a rope attached to a hook in the ceiling. After the inquest the lady gave up the house.

"It was then closed up for some time, but was again advertised 'To let,' and a caretaker, a woman, was put into it. One night about one o'clock, a constable going his rounds heard someone calling for help from the house, and found the caretaker on the sill of one of the windows holding on as best she could. He told her to go in and open the hall door and let him in, but she refused to enter the room again. He forced open the door and succeeded in dragging the woman back into the room, only to find she had gone mad.

"Again the house was shut up, and again it was let, this time to a lady, on a five-years' lease. However, after a few months' residence, she locked it up, and went away. On her friends asking her why she did so, she replied that she would rather pay the whole five years' rent than live in it herself, or allow anyone else to do so, but would give no other reason.

"'I believe I was the next person to take this house,' said the lady who narrated the story to me (*i.e.* Mr. de Lacy). 'I took it about eighteen months ago on a three-years' lease in the hopes of making money by taking in boarders, but I am now giving it up because none of them will stay more than a week or two. They do not give any definite reason as to why they are leaving; they are careful to state that it is not because they have any fault to find with me or my domestic arrangements, but they merely say *they do not like the rooms!* The rooms themselves, as you can see, are good, spacious, and well lighted. I have had all classes of professional men; one of the last was a barrister, and he said that he had no fault to find except that *he did not like the rooms!* I myself do not believe in ghosts, and I have never seen anything strange here or elsewhere; and if I had known the house had the reputation of being haunted, I would never have rented it.'"

Marsh's library, that quaint, old-world repository of ponderous tomes, is reputed to be haunted by the ghost of its founder, Primate Narcissus Marsh. He is said to frequent the inner gallery, which contains what was formerly his own private library: he moves in and out among the cases, taking down books from the shelves, and occasionally throwing them down on the reader's desk as if in anger. However, he always leaves things in perfect order. The late Mr. —— who for some years lived in the librarian's rooms underneath, was a firm believer in this ghost, and said he frequently heard noises which could only be accounted for by the presence of a nocturnal visitor; the present tenant is more sceptical. The story goes that Marsh's niece eloped from the Palace, and was married in a tavern to the curate of Chapelizod. She is reported to have written a note consenting to the elopement, and to have then placed it in one of her uncle's books to which her lover had access, and where he found it. As a punishment for his lack of vigilance, the Archbishop is said to be condemned to hunt for the note until he find it—hence the ghost.

The ghost of a deceased Canon was seen in one of the Dublin cathedrals by several independent witnesses, one of whom, a lady, gives her own experience as follows: "Canon—— was a personal friend of mine, and we had many times discussed ghosts and spiritualism, in which he was a profound believer, having had many supernatural experiences himself. It was during the Sunday morning service in the cathedral that I saw my friend, who had been dead for two years, sitting inside the communion-rails. I was so much astonished at the flesh-and-blood appearance of the figure that I took off my glasses and wiped them with my handkerchief, at the same time looking away from him down the church. On looking back again he was still there, and continued to sit there for about ten or twelve minutes, after which he faded away. I remarked a change in his personal appearance, which was, that his beard was longer and whiter than when I had known him—in fact, such a change as would have occurred *in life* in the space of two years. Having told my husband of the occurrence on our way home, he remembered having heard some talk of an appearance of this clergyman in the robestress if anybody had seen Canon ——'s ghost. She informed him that *she* had, and that he had also been seen by one of the sextons in the cathedral. I mention this because in describing his personal appearance she had remarked the same change as I had with regard to the beard."

Some years ago a family had very uncanny experiences in a house in Rathgar, and subsequently in another in Rathmines. These were communicated by one of the young ladies to Mrs. M. A. Wilkins, who published them in the *Journal of the American S.P.R.*,[1] from which they are here taken. The Rathgar house had a basement passage leading to a door into the yard, and along this passage her mother and the children used to hear dragging, limping steps, and the latch of the door rattling, but no one could ever be found when search was made. The house-bells were old and all in a row, and on one occasion they all rang, apparently of their own accord. The lady narrator used to sleep in the back drawing room, and always when the light was put out she heard strange noises, as if someone was going round the room rubbing paper along the wall, while she often had the feeling that a person was standing beside her bed. A cousin, who was a nurse, once slept with her, and also noticed these strange noises. On one occasion this room was given up to a

[1] For September 1913.

very matter-of-fact young man to sleep in, and next morning he said that the room was very strange, with queer noises in it.

Her mother also had an extraordinary experience in the same house. One evening she had just put the baby to bed, when she heard a voice calling "mother." She left the bedroom, and called to her daughter, who was in a lower room, "What do you want?" But the girl replied that she had *not* called her; and then, in her turn, asked her mother if *she* had been in the front room, for she had just heard a noise as if someone was trying to fasten the inside bars of the shutters across. But her mother had been upstairs, and no one was in the front room. The experiences in the Rathmines house were of a similar auditory nature, *i.e.* the young ladies heard their names called, though it was found that no one in the house had done so.

Occasionally it happens that ghosts inspire a law-suit. In the seventeenth century they were to be found actively urging the adoption of legal proceedings, but in the nineteenth and twentieth centuries they play a more passive part. A case about a haunted house took place in Dublin in the year 1885, in which the ghost may be said to have won. A Mr. Waldron, a solicitor's clerk, sued his next-door neighbour, one Mr. Kiernan, a mate in the merchant service, to recover £500 for damages done to his house.

Kiernan altogether denied the charges, but asserted that Waldron's house was notoriously haunted. Witnesses proved that every night, from August 1884 to January 1885, stones were thrown at the windows and doors, and extraordinary and inexplicable occurrences constantly took place.

Mrs. Waldron, wife of the plaintiff, swore that one night she saw one of the panes of glass of a certain window cut through with a diamond, and a white hand inserted through the hole. She at once caught up a bill-hook and aimed a blow at the hand, cutting off one of the fingers. This finger could not be found, nor were any traces of blood seen.

A servant of hers was sorely persecuted by noises and the sound of footsteps. Mr. Waldron, with the aid of detectives and policemen, endeavoured to find out the cause, but with no success. The witnesses in the case were closely cross-examined, but without shaking their testimony. The facts appeared to be proved, so the jury found for Kiernan, the defendant. At least twenty persons had testified on oath to the fact that the house had been known to have been haunted.[2]

Before leaving the city and its immediate surroundings, we must relate the story of an extraordinary ghost, somewhat lacking in good manners, yet not without a certain distorted sense of humour. Absolutely incredible though the tale may seem, yet it comes on very good authority. It was related to our informant, Mr. D., by a Mrs. C., whose daughter he had employed as governess. Mrs. C., who is described as "a woman of respectable position and good education," heard it in her turn from her father and mother. In the story the relationship of the different persons seems a little involved, but it would appear that the initial A belongs to the surname both of Mrs. C.'s father and grandfather.

This ghost was commonly called "Corney" by the family, and he answered to this though it was not his proper name. He disclosed this latter to Mr. C.'s mother, who forgot it. Corney made his presence manifest to the A— family shortly after they had gone to reside in —— Street in the following manner. Mr. A— had sprained his knee badly, and had to use a crutch, which

---

2   See *Sights and Shadows*, p.42 ff.

at night was left at the head of his bed. One night his wife heard someone walking on the lobby, thump, thump, thump, as if imitating Mr. A—. She struck a match to see if the crutch had been removed from the head of the bed, but it was still there.

From that on Corney commenced to talk, and he spoke every day from his usual habitat, the coal-cellar off the kitchen. His voice sounded as if it came out of an empty barrel.

He was very troublesome, and continually played practical jokes on the servants, who, as might be expected, were in terror of their lives of him; so much so that Mrs. A— could hardly induce them to stay with her. They used to sleep in a press-bed in the kitchen, and in order to get away from Corney, they asked for a room at the top of the house, which was given to them. Accordingly the press-bed was moved up there. The first night they went to retire to bed after the change, the doors of the press were flung open, and Corney's voice said, "Ha! Ha! You devils, I am here before you! I am not confined to any particular part of this house."

Corney was continually tampering with the doors, and straining locks and keys. He only manifested himself in material form to two persons; to ——, who died with the fright, and to Mr. A— (Mrs. C.'s father) when he was about seven years old. The latter described him to his mother as a naked man, with a curl on his forehead, and a skin like a clothes-horse (!).

One day a servant was preparing fish for dinner. She laid it on the kitchen table while she went elsewhere for something she wanted. When she returned the fish had disappeared. She thereupon began to cry, fearing she would be accused of making away with it. The next thing she heard was the voice of Corney from the coal-cellar saying, "There, you blubbering fool, is your fish for you!" and, suiting the action to the word, the fish was thrown out on the kitchen floor.

Relatives from the country used to bring presents of vegetables, and these were often hung up by Corney like Christmas decorations round the kitchen. There was one particular press in the kitchen he would not allow anything into. He would throw it out again. A crock with meat in pickle was put into it, and a fish placed on the cover of the crock. He threw the fish out.

Silver teaspoons were missing, and no account of them could be got until Mrs. A— asked Corney to confess if he had done anything with them. He said, "They are under the ticking in the servants' bed." He had, so he said, a daughter in —— Street, and sometimes announced that he was going to see her, and would not be here to-night.

On one occasion he announced that he was going to have "company" that evening, and if they wanted any water out of the soft-water tank, to take it before going to bed, as he and his friends would be using it. Subsequently that night five or six distinct voices were heard, and next morning the water in the tank was as black as ink, and not alone that, but the bread and butter in the pantry were streaked with the marks of sooty fingers.

A clergyman in the locality, having heard of the doings of Corney, called to investigate the matter. He was advised by Mrs. A— to keep quiet, and not to reveal his identity, as being the best chance of hearing Corney speak. He waited a long time, and as the capricious Corney remained silent, he left at length. The servants asked, "Corney, why did you not speak?" and he replied, "I could not speak while that good man was in the house." The servants sometimes used to ask him where he was. He would reply, "The Great God would not permit me to tell you. I was a bad man, and I died the death." He named the room in the house in which he died.

Corney constantly joined in any conversation carried on by the people of the house. One could never tell when a voice from the coal-cellar would erupt into the dialogue. He had his likes and dislikes: he appeared to dislike anyone that was not afraid of him, and would not talk to them. Mrs. C.'s mother, however, used to get good of him by coaxing. An uncle, having failed to get him to speak one night, took the kitchen poker, and hammered at the door of the coal-cellar, saying, "I'll make you speak"; but Corney wouldn't. Next morning the poker was found broken in two. This uncle used to wear spectacles, and Corney used to call him derisively, "Four-eyes." An uncle named Richard came to sleep one night, and complained in the morning that the clothes were pulled off him. Corney told the servants in great glee, "I slept on Master Richard's feet all night."

Finally Mr. A— made several attempts to dispose of his lease, but with no success, for when intending purchasers were being shown over the house and arrived at Corney's domain, the spirit would begin to speak and the would-be purchaser would fly. They asked him if they changed house would he trouble them. He replied, "No! But if they throw down this house, I will trouble the stones."

At last Mrs. A— appealed to him to keep quiet, and not to injure people who had never injured him. He promised that he would do so, and then said, "Mrs. A—, you will be all right now, for I see a lady in black coming up the street to this house, and she will buy it." Within half an hour a widow called and purchased the house. Possibly Corney is still there, for our informant looked up the Directory as he was writing, and found the house marked "Vacant."

Near Blanchardstown, Co. Dublin, is a house, occupied at present, or up to very recently, by a private family; it was formerly a monastery, and there are said to be secret passages in it. Once a servant ironing in the kitchen saw the figure of a nun approach the kitchen window and look in. Our informant was also told by a friend (now dead), who had it from the lady of the house, that once night falls, no doors can be kept closed. If anyone shuts them, almost immediately they are flung open again with the greatest violence and apparent anger. If left open there is no trouble or noise, but light footsteps are heard, and there is a vague feeling of people passing to and fro. The persons inhabiting the house are matter-of-fact, unimaginative people, who speak of this as if it were an everyday affair. "So long as we leave the doors unclosed they don't harm us: why should we be afraid of them?" Mrs.—— said. Truly a most philosophical attitude to adopt!

A haunted house in Kingstown, Co. Dublin, was investigated by Professor W. Barrett and Professor Henry Sidgwick. The story is singularly well attested (as one might expect from its being inserted in the pages of the *Proceedings* S.P.R.[3]), as the apparition was seen on three distinct occasions, and by three separate persons who were all personally known to the above gentlemen. The house in which the following occurrences took place is described as being a very old one, with unusually thick walls. The lady saw her strange visitant in her bedroom. She says: "Disliking cross-lights, I had got into the habit of having the blind of the back window drawn and the shutters closed at night, and of leaving the blind raised and the shutters opened towards the front, liking to see the trees and sky when I awakened. Opening my eyes now one morning, I saw right before me (this occurred in July 1873) the figure of a woman, stooping down and apparently looking at me. Her head and shoulders were wrapped in a common woollen shawl; her arms were folded,

---

[3]   1 July 1884, p. 141.

and they were also wrapped, as if for warmth, in the shawl. I looked at her in my horror, and dared not cry out lest I might move the awful thing to speech or action. Behind her head I saw the window and the growing dawn, the looking-glass upon the toilet-table, and the furniture in that part of the room. After what may have been only seconds—of the duration of this vision I cannot judge—she raised herself and went backwards towards the window, stood at the toilet-table, and gradually vanished. I mean she grew by degrees transparent, and that through the shawl and the grey dress she wore I saw the white muslin of the table-cover again, and at last saw that only in the place where she had stood." The lady lay motionless with terror until the servant came to call her. The only other occupants of the house at the time were her brother and the servant, to neither of whom did she make any mention of the circumstance, fearing that the former would laugh at her, and the latter give notice.

Exactly a fortnight later, when sitting at breakfast, she noticed that her brother seemed out of sorts, and did not eat. On asking him if anything were the matter, he answered, "I have had a horrid nightmare—indeed it was no nightmare: I saw it early this morning, just as distinctly as I see you." "What?" she asked. "A villainous-looking hag," he replied, "with her head and arms wrapped in a cloak, stooping over me, and looking like this—" He got up, folded his arms, and put himself in the exact posture of the vision. Whereupon she informed him of what she herself had seen a fortnight previously.

About four years later, in the same month, the lady's married sister and two children were alone in the house. The eldest child, a boy of about four or five years, asked for a drink, and his mother went to fetch it, desiring him to remain in the dining-room until her return. Coming back she met the boy pale and trembling, and on asking him why he left the room, he replied, "Who is that woman—who is that woman?" "Where?" she asked. "That old woman who went upstairs," he replied. So agitated was he, that she took him by the hand and went upstairs to search, but no one was to be found, though he still maintained that a woman went upstairs. A friend of the family subsequently told them that a woman had been killed in the house many years previously, and that it was reported to be haunted.

A lady sends a very curious account of the appearance of an archiepiscopal ghost in a house in the outskirts of Dublin. Those of my readers who are acquainted with that Archbishop's family history will be able to say if some of the facts related below are correct.

A good many years ago a Mrs. P., an intimate friend of the narrator, lived in Upper Fitzwilliam Street. Her husband had held the post of Government arbitrator, and was subsequently agent to a large estate. During his lifetime he and his wife resided at a house near Dundrum, Co. Dublin, a great rambling old mansion, which has since suffered of the fate of so many stately houses, as it has become a teaching establishment of some sort.

One afternoon, when it was getting dusk, Mrs. P. was descending the large staircase when she saw going down before her what she imagined to be her youngest son, W., curiously attired. She had three sons, all of whom were very fond of amateur theatricals, and from the dress that W. wore she thought that he was about to take part in some rehearsal. He was clad in a large broad brimmed sombrero, and a cloak put on in Spanish fashion. She called to him by name, bidding him wait for her, but to her surprise he took absolutely no notice, but continued descending, she following him, until he reached the door of the dining-room, which he entered. She was quite annoyed at his want of manners, and followed him into the dining-room, an apartment which they did not always use because it was very large. To her astonishment she found herself confronted, not by her son, but by an utter stranger who had walked to the far side of the dining-table, and there stood facing her. His cloak was pulled up so as to cover his mouth, and his hat drawn well down over his face, and on this account Mrs. P. was unable to distinguish his features, but she could see that his eyes were looking at her. Then he walked a little round the table, and suddenly vanished. Mrs. P. got a great shock, but her sons, when they heard it, attributed it to imagination pure and simple.

"I had heard this story many times and never paid much heed to it," continued our narrator. "However, one day I went to a Loreto Convent to visit some nuns of my acquaintance who were there for their holidays, and while there the conversation turned on the subject of ghosts. I related the story I have just told to you. One of the nuns present asked if she might bring in another nun to hear the story; this latter was a Rev. Mother of an English House who was over for her holiday. I was quite agreeable, so this Rev. Mother was introduced, and to her I told my tale again. She seemed more than usually interested, and said she would particularly like to meet Mrs. P., if it were possible, and would I ask her to try and recall the exact day and date on which she had seen the figure in the dining-room.

"I made an arrangement with Mrs. P., and brought her to the convent, where she met this Rev. Mother, to whom she related to her experience, giving day and date, and almost the exact hour. From the subsequent conversation I learnt that this Rev. Mother was a niece, or some near relative, of the celebrated Archbishop Whately; she had turned Roman Catholic, and had entered a Loreto Convent. The Archbishop had owned this old mansion where Mrs. P. had lived, and had resided there for some time. It was said that he used to appear there whenever any near relative of his died. On ascertaining the day and date of the appearance to Mrs. P., the Rev. Mother was able to say that exactly at that time her cousin, a daughter (I think) of the Archbishop's, had passed away. He had been in Spain and had brought back from there the sombrero and a cloak which he fancied very much. Thus the theatrically-clad figure which was seen by my friend there was none other than the Archbishop himself."

A much more unpleasant haunting was experienced by Mrs. E. H. B. and her daughters in a house on of the south side of Dublin.[4]

"This house was a large, sunny, rambling old place, not the least like the typical 'haunted house.' Our two girls occupied a very large room at the back of the house, little F. being a hopeless invalid, and needing someone to sleep in her room.

"We had been there about a week, and we had just gone to bed, when M.(our eldest girl) rushed wildly into our room crying: 'Mother, there is something rushing about in our bedroom, and we can't see it, and F. is so frightened—do come!'

"I ran down at once, and on the stairs I could distinctly hear something jumping about in the room, the door of which was open. Before we got in, however, the noise stopped, but I promised I would stay with them all night, for poor little F. could not speak, and clung to me convulsively.

"At last all was quiet, the girls slept, when I heard in one corner of the room a soft, sighing, whispering sound, which seemed to come out of the wall, and gradually crept all round the room until it reached where our beds were. Nearer it came, till it touched the bed, as if a winged beetle were fluttering against the quilt. All at once something heavy seemed to fall, and immediately the footfalls I had heard before sounded with a peculiar hollow thud,

---

4 *Occult Review*, vol. iii. p.19.

as if some animal (cat or dog) were jumping up and down; it lasted about ten minutes, and suddenly died away at the door. Next morning both girls exactly described the first part of the noise as I had heard it, and it always came in the same way—an indescribable whisper in the beginning, and the conclusion a heavy thud.

"But next day we had a visit from a friend (!), a pet aversion of ours, whose presence always put little sensitive F. into a fever. I subsequently noticed that whenever this person came to see us we always received a visit overnight from the 'Pronc' (a name F. gave to the 'thuddy' sounds of our ghost), as if it knew that some evil was on its way to us, and was drawn to the spot by its magnetic influence. Indeed after a visit from the 'Pronc' I always stayed in next day to be on the spot and protect the children.

"One evening I was sitting in the firelight by F.'s bed, telling her stories, as I often did, when she gripped my hand, and nodded towards the fire. I looked round. There on the rug, with its back to us, sat a black animal, like a large tom-cat, gazing into the fire! I thought it was F.'s pet cat, and called out, 'Well, Peter-Puss! Are you come in for your supper?' The creature turned, and looked full at us for a moment *with eyes that were human*, and a face which, though black, was still the face of an *ugly woman*! The mouth snarled at us for an instant, and a sad, angry howl came from it; and as we stared in horror, the thing vanished. We never saw it again, but the strain was too much, and we left the house as soon as we could. We were told later that fifty years before a woman had been robbed and murdered in that room by her son, and buried by him under the hearthstone! Twenty years after, her skeleton was found by tenants, who were troubled by the ghost, searched the house, and gave their gruesome find decent burial."

II

HAUNTED HOUSES IN CONN'S HALF

F ROM a very early period a division of Ireland into two "halves" existed. This was traditionally believed to have been made by Conn the Hundred-fighter and Mogh Nuadat, in A.D. 166. The north was in consequence known as Conn's Half, the south as Mogh's Half, the line of division being a series of gravel hills extending from Dublin to Galway. This division we have followed, except that we have included the whole of the counties of Westmeath and Galway in the northern portion. We had hoped originally to have had four chapters on Haunted Houses, one for each of the four provinces, but, for lack of material from Connaught, we have been forced to adopt the plan on which Chapters I–III are arranged.

Mrs. Acheson, of Co. Roscommon, sends the following: "Emo House, Co. Westmeath, a very old mansion since pulled down, was purchased by my grandfather for his son, my father. The latter had only been living in it for a few days when knocking commenced at the hall door. Naturally he thought it was someone playing tricks, or endeavouring to frighten him away. One night he had the lobby window open directly over the door. The knocking commenced, and he looked out: it was a very bright night, and as there was no porch he could see the door distinctly;

the knocking continued, but he did not see the knocker move. Another night he sat up expecting his brother, but as the latter did not come he went to bed. Finally the knocking became so loud and insistent that he felt sure his brother must have arrived. He went downstairs and opened the door, but no one was there. Still convinced that his brother was there and had gone round to the yard to put up his horse, he went out; but scarcely had he gone twenty yards from the door when the knocking recommenced behind his back. On turning round he could see no one.

"After this the knocking got very bad, so much so that he could not rest. All this time he did not mention the strange occurrence to anyone. One morning he went up through the fields between four and five o'clock. To his surprise he found the herd out feeding the cattle. My father asked him why he was up so early. He replied that he could not sleep. 'Why?' asked my father. 'You know why yourself, sir—the knocking.' He then found that this man had heard it all the time, though he slept at the end of a long house. My father was advised to take no notice of it, for it would go as it came, though at this time it was continuous and very loud; and so it did. The country people said it was the late resident who could not rest.

"We had another curious and most eerie experience in this house. A former rector was staying the night with us, and as the evening wore on we commenced to tell ghost-stories. He related some remarkable experiences, and as we were talking the drawing-room door suddenly opened as wide as possible, and then slowly closed again. It was a calm night, and at any rate it was a heavy double door which never flies open however strong the wind may be blowing. Everyone in the house was in bed, as it was after 12 o'clock, except the three persons who witnessed this, viz. myself, my daughter, and the rector. The effect on the latter was most marked. He was a big, strong, jovial man and a good athlete, but when he saw the door open he quivered like an aspen leaf."

A lady, who desires to have names of persons and places suppressed, sends a tale of a haunted hotel.

"DEAR SIR

"I have been reading your very interesting book, *True Irish Ghost Stories*, and I thought I would send you an account of an apparition that once appeared to my mother. In the month of November in the year 1895 my father's regiment was send from Belfast to Mullingar. My father, who was Canteen Steward, went with the advance party to make preparations for the arrival of the regiment. My father, my mother, and myself—I was then a girl of fourteen—stayed at a certain hotel in Mullingar. As it was the week of a fair the hotel was very crowded, and I was given a stretcher to sleep on, which was placed in a corner of the room occupied by my parents. My mother told me that some time during the night she woke up with a great feeling of fear, and sat up in bed. The room was in total darkness, but in the corner where I was lying asleep there appeared to be a strange kind of light, and she distinctly saw a table with a man sitting at it, looking very pale and frightened; he was in his shirt-sleeves, but, as she watched, the vision slowly faded, and the room became quiet again. My mother got out of bed, and walked over to me; she then raised the blind and looked out of the window, but there was positively nothing to account for what she had seen. She told my father about it, but he laughed and said it was all nonsense. Some time afterwards in a laughing manner she happened to mention the ghost to the people who owned the hotel. They all looked very serious, and spoke of a man who had been shot as a spy by the Fenians. He was a commercial traveller, but the Fenians believed him to be a spy. That is my story—and to the day of her death my mother always solemnly declared she had seen that vision. The last time I was in the hotel I noticed that that particular room had been cleared of its furniture and was used as a lumber-room.—

Yours very truly,
"Oct. 31, 1915."

The Rev. Leslie G. Davis, Rector of Castle Connell, Co. Limerick, thus describes his experiences some years ago in a haunted house in the north.

"When I had just taken my degree in T.C.D., some close friends of mine invited me in July on a visit to their home in the North of Ireland. Their house was in a small town, and looked out on the harbour. A few days after my arrival a small dance was given by some of my friends, to which we all went, returning home a little after midnight. For that particular night I had given up my usual bedroom to another visitor, and I slept on a stretcher in a tiny smoking-room at the top of the first flight of stairs. This toom had one door, one window, and no fireplace. When I retired to my room I locked the door, and in less than no time was in bed and fast asleep. Suddenly I awoke, feeling most plainly two hands pressing upon my knees, and then gradually passing up my body until one was on my shoulder and the other on my chin. Needless to say, by this time I was very wide awake indeed, and almost paralysed with terror. With a sudden movement I pulled the bedclothes right up over my head; in about half a minute I flung them off again, made a grab for the box of matches and candlestick which were on a table beside the bed. I lit the candle as quickly as possible, and then got up and made a searching examination of the room. Everything was as I had left it when going to bed; the door was still locked, the window was as it had been, namely, open at the top for three or four inches, and the blind pulled down. There was nothing which could in any way explain my experience. I went back to bed, but left the candle burning till daylight appeared.

"At the breakfast-table next morning I related my very unpleasant experience to my hosts. They laughed at me, and made unsympathetic remarks about nightmares, indigestion, etc. But when they thought I was not observing them I noticed significant glances passing between them!

"On either the first or the second Sunday after this episode I had been to church in the morning, and decided not to go in the evening. My hostess and her family all went, so did the two servants, while the old family nurse—familiarly known as 'Granny'—who was a Methodist, went to her own place of worship. So I was left all alone in the house, a three-storey building. It was a glorious bright July evening. I sat in the drawing-room, which was on the second floor, in an armchair which I had placed between the fireplace and one of the windows; as it happened, I was facing the door, which was wide open. So intent was I on reading that I let my pipe go out. Just as I was in the act of relighting it I saw most plainly the figure of an old woman, dressed in black clothes of a very old-fashioned make, walk past the open door. Very much surprised, and assuming it to be 'Granny,' I called out to her, but received no reply, and thought she must have gone to her room on the third floor. In a few moments, however, the figure repassed the drawing-room door. Again, I called 'Granny,' and again I received no reply. This behaviour being quite unlike that of dear old 'Granny,' I got up and followed downstairs, getting a third glimpse of the figure as it turned into the dining-room. I went into the room after her, but no one was to be seen there. Later on, when the real 'Granny' returned, I opened the hall door for her and questioned her as to why she had come so quietly into the house some little time before, and gently chided her for not answering my greeting. She informed me that she had only just left the Chapel, where she had been for over an hour. This I afterwards found to be correct.

"It was not until after my experiences in this house that my friends told me that they frequently saw this ghost. The daughters had small pet dogs, which slept in their bedroom on the third floor. Sometimes the dogs would wake them up by their barking, and there—standing by the window, with elbow on the sill, gazing out to sea—they would see this apparition. The house in which these things happened was a very old one. I never succeeded in finding the facts of its history, but some thought that at one time it had been an inn, and that murder had been committed there."

A strange story of a haunting, in which nothing was seen, but in which the same noises were heard by different people, is sent by one of the percipients, who does not wish to have her name disclosed. She says: "When staying for a time in a country house in the North of Ireland some years ago I was awakened on several nights by hearing the tramp, tramp, of horses' hoofs. Sometimes it sounded as if they were walking on paving-stones, while at other times I had the impression that they were going round a large space, and as if someone was using a whip on them. I heard neighing, and champing of bits, and so formed the impression that they were carriage horses. I did not mind it much at first, as I thought the stables must be near that part of the house. After hearing these noises several times I began to get curious, so one morning I made a tour of the place. I found that the side of the house I occupied overlooked a neglected garden, which was mostly used for drying clothes. I also discovered that the stables were right at the back of the house, and so it would be impossible for me to hear any noises in that quarter; at any rate there was only one farm horse left, and this was securely fastened up every night. Also there were no cobble-stones round the yard. I mentioned what I had heard to the people of the house, but as they would give me no satisfactory reply I passed it over. I did not hear these noises every night.

"One night I was startled out of my sleep by hearing a dreadful disturbance in the kitchen. It sounded as if the dish-covers were being taken off the wall and dashed violently on the flagged floor. At length I got up and opened the door of my bedroom, and just as I did so an appalling crash resounded through the house. I waited to see if there was any light to be seen, or footstep to be heard, but nobody was stirring. There was only one servant in the house, the other persons being my host, his wife, and a baby, who had all retired early. Next morning I described the noises in the kitchen to the servant, and she said she had often heard them. I then told her about the tramping of horses: she replied that she herself had never heard it, but that other persons who had occupied my room had had experiences similar to mine. I asked her was there any explanation; she said no, except that a story was told of a gentleman who had lived there some years ago, and was very much addicted to racing and gambling, and that he was shot one night in that house. For the remainder of my visit I was removed to another part of the house, and I heard no more noises."

A lady sends the following account of her experiences in a small house in Co. Mayo.

"I saw some little time ago in the *Irish Times* that you were about to compile a book of ghost stories, and that brought back to my mind a strange experience which befell my late husband and myself some years ago when living in the West of Ireland. He was then Resident Engineer to the Collooney and Claremorris Railway, then in process of construction. We took a small cottage about three-quarters of a mile outside the town, and a little off the main road. All the engineers and contractors used to meet once a month in one of the hotels in the town in order to talk over what had been done, and to compare notes; this was called 'Certificate Night.' When the business was concluded there was generally some exchange of ideas, and perhaps a game of cards. I never waited up for my husband, not knowing when the sitting would be over.

"One night, when we had been in the cottage some time, I went to bed as usual and fell asleep. Once cannot keep count of the hours when one is asleep, but after a while I was awakened by hearing a footstep cross my sitting-room, which was outside our bedroom, and then come into the bedroom itself—a hand was laid on my shoulder! I sat up wide awake, and at once concluded that my husband had returned from the meeting. I always left the hall-door on the latch so that he might be able to get in whenever he liked. I said 'What is the matter?' but got no reply. Again I heard the footsteps cross the sitting-room, and a voice I did not recognise saying, 'Good-night! Good-night!' I thought it must be my husband trying to frighten me, as he had often heard me say I believed in the supernatural and would not be afraid of a ghost; so I imagined that he was anxious to test my courage.

"Again I fell asleep, I cannot say for how long, when I was again awakened by a tap at the window—all the windows were on the ground floor—and I heard my husband's voice saying,

'Will you open the hall-door and let me in, as it is fastened.' I got up at once and let him in, very angry at being disturbed a second time. I said, 'What on earth possessed you to come in and touch me, and then go out again?' He only looked at me with a queer smile and said, 'What have you been having for supper? It must have given you a nightmare!'

"After that many queer things happened. Knocks would come to the bedroom door, but when we opened it there would be no one there. Sometimes we would hear sounds as if the kitchen fire was being violently poked; but it was a turf fire, and so never needed poking. Also we heard shouting—both of us would awake at the same instant, each thinking the other was calling. The one servant we had slept in an attic over the kitchen, approached by a ladder which she carefully drew up after she had retired, so she knew nothing of what I am telling you, nor did either of us mention it to her.

"One day we went to call on an old friend, who was doctor a good many miles off. We went in the morning, and he insisted on our staying for lunch; and while it was being prepared suggested that we should go for a little walk. On our way we passed the gates of a seemingly deserted house, with a fine avenue all covered with weeds and dark overhanging boughs. I said to him, 'I am always hearing that houses are hard to be got round here—why isn't this one occupied?' 'Oh!' he replied, 'there are queer stories about that house. No one ever stays long in it. In the course of my professional duties I am often called out at night, and I prefer to go a good bit out of the way on my road home rather than pass those gates.' He then mentioned one or two things about the house, saying that it was reported to be haunted.

"I listened to him, and when he had finished speaking, I said, 'You have told me queer things. Now I shall tell you of our experiences at the cottage'; whereupon I related what I have just written. When I had finished my story he shook his head, and said, 'I don't wonder! I had a great friend, a cultured man, who was an inspector of national schools. He used to come round here periodically and put up at the cottage; and when he did he used always to send over for me to come and dine, and spend a pleasant evening with him. About two years ago he came as usual, writing to me beforehand to say what day to expect him. I went accordingly in anticipation of the pleasure his visit always gave me. But I found him silent and morose, not at all like his usual pleasant self. He ate nothing, nor did he drink anything, and after the meal was over we sat in silence by the fireside, having a smoke, which he did not seem to enjoy either. At length I became weary of doing and saying nothing, so rising and pushing back my chair, I said, 'My dear fellow, was is wrong with you? I never saw you in such a mood before! You won't eat, drink, nor talk! Why,' I added in jest, 'you seem like a man who is contemplating suicide! I am going home, and hope that next time we meet you will be better company!' So saying I bade him adieu, mounted my horse, and rode off. I had barely reached home when a messenger came hot foot after me to say my poor friend had put an end to himself, and would I see if I could do anything for him. I returned as quickly as I could, and on arriving at the cottage found that he had cut his throat, and was beyond the reach of human aid.'

"My husband, who was walking on the other side of the doctor, at this leant across with a queer little smile, and said to me, 'I heard in the town, when first we took that cottage, that strange things used to happen there, but I was warned not to tell you lest you should be frightened. Also if we spread storied about the house the landlady would have cause to complain that we had spoiled her chances of letting it.' So he knew all the time, but kept his own counsel! We stayed on in the cottage for a good while after that, and got quite used to knockings and other strange noises."

An extraordinary and varied group of personal experiences, occurring in the West of Ireland, is related by Mrs. Ada Vere Hunt, of Ardmayle House, Co. Tipperary.

"The house in which I spent my childhood was haunted—or perhaps it would be more correct to say that the entire district was and is haunted. The house to which I refer was a one storey building, with a wide terrace running along the front, while the sea surrounded it on three sides. Two flights of steps led up to the house, one in the front, and the other in the rear. My bedroom was at the back, with French windows opening beside the steps.

"Atlantic gales often blew, and struck the trees and gables with their full fury, yet even if the storm raged its fiercest—and it *can* blow there at times—not a single night passed without my hearing the sound of a footstep on the topmost flag of the flight beside my room. I never felt frightened at it, as it seemed quite a friendly sound! However, one summer the single stepped changed to running footsteps. Every night someone seemed to run round the end of the house, and then stumble up the steps. I told my father about this, and he determined to investigate the matter. He sat up one night in the room next to mine, and I sat up too, waiting for the footsteps. The moment I heard them commencing I called to him. He dashed out through the French window, but could see nothing. All the family laughed at me, and put it down to imagination. However, on the following night, as soon as I heard the sound running, I hastened to the window myself, and on drawing aside the blind encountered the angry gaze of the queerest little old woman who seemed to be dragging a box after her by a string. Curiously enough, that was the end of it; never again did I hear the running or the footstep.

"The path round the gable of the house went sloping up to encircle a high garden at the back, which had on the other side a steep bank falling some hundred feet down to the road wall. I was possessed of insatiable curiosity in those days, and never had any hesitation about rushing out in the dark to investigate anything strange. At about eleven o'clock at night we used to hear a horse and trap coming along the road below the garden. We often went to see who was travelling so late, but this was always a most unsatisfactory proceeding. We could hear the car coming along steadily, and just as we expected to catch sight of it there was silence and an empty road! After a minute or two there would come the sound of wheels and hoofs rapidly receding in the other direction, as if the car had passed by us on its journey. Yet the road had lain empty under our eyes all the time!

"An experience which I had one autumn afternoon was truly terrifying. A day of easterly gale and rain had ended in a dead calm; the sun set in ragged swirls of red and black clouds, and cast a gleaming track on the oily swell of the waters. I left the house to go to the post office, which was about half a mile away, on a road which was bordered on one side by the sea, and on the other by a hilly farm. There were ten children at the post office, and when I drew near it, and heard a child crying, I thought one of them must be hurt, so I called out the names of as many of the children as I could remember, asking them if they were hurt. I received no answer, only the wailing became more pitiful. So I called out again, 'Whoever you are, come over here and answer me!' I was leaning over the wall that bounded the farm, looking for the child, when all at once the crying rose like the swell of a great organ, and enveloped me in a deafening inferno of sound.

I was flung clean across the road, and found myself clinging to the sea-wall and listening to the sound as it swept over the sea, growing ever fainter and fainter until at last it died away altogether. I fell on the road, and after a little got up and made my way to the post office, where everything seemed to be all right. However, the next day I was at the farmhouse on the hillside, and found them in terrible trouble. 'My grand little girl of a grand-daughter was burnt at a bonfire in Liverpool, and we got a telegram to say she died,' the old woman told me. I inquired if they knew the hour the tragedy had occurred, and was told five o'clock, which was just the time I had heard the crying.

"Some time later we moved to a house near a mill which was not worked, and by which ran an avenue known as Mill Road. This road was reputed to be haunted, and the hill behind the house had an Irish name which meant 'the hill of the headless man.' The whole place, house and garden, had an air of calm repose, yet it was on the Mill Road that I had my next experience. One summer evening I was walking up alone from the front gate to the house. Just as I was passing the empty mill I began to be afraid, and felt that something was moving beside me—some terrible malignant Thing that was willing me to look at it. I had a most intense struggle with myself not to do so: this strong will at time almost overpowered mine, yet I felt that if I yielded to it and looked, something awful would happen to me. At length I reached the garden-gate, where I met my mother. 'Who was the man in black who was walking beside you?' she asked. 'We all saw him coming up, and thought it was Mr. B., and then he seemed to vanish!' I never met the man in black again, I am glad to say, but on the same avenue I had another experience. I was walking on it one sunny morning with three gentlemen friends when I heard a woman sobbing so loudly and bitterly that I could scarcely catch my friends' conversation. I felt that it did not concern me personally; a little later I learnt that the young brother of one of my companions was killed in France that day.

"I shall now relate to you my last, and I think most peculiar and inexplicable experience. The hills and valleys of the West are teeming with legends, especially the boggy plateau behind Croagh Patrick, wherein is the reputed dwelling of the River-horse. I was once on the summit of that mountain with two friends at a time when some workmen were engaged on the chapel there. It was a glorious June day, very calm, with brilliant sunshine and perfect visibility. Lough Nacorra lay far below us to the south, an unruffled glassy sheet, with the cattle only like tiny dots on the shore.

"Suddenly the surface of the water was disturbed by a huge black shape that rose and swam the length of the lake in what appeared to be a few movements. Other similar shapes than appeared, and all these weird things kept playing about, diving and swimming like a lot of seals. The lake is between two and three miles long, and from the height on which we were, and in comparison with the cattle, the creatures looked bigger than any house we could see: even with the aid of binoculars we could not distinguish any details at that distance; we could only see the black monsters playing about. We called to the men who were working at the chapel to come and watch. After a short time the creatures disappeared one by one, and the lake resumed its former tranquil appearance. I have never been given any explanation of what we three, and ten or twelve others, saw on that June day, and would very much like to have one."

Another curious story of mysterious footsteps and ringing of bells was related to the present writer by a friend, Mr. Richard Pearson, of Doon, Co. Limerick. He describes his experience as follows:

"In the year 1914 I went to study practical farming under a Mr. B., who lived near the town of Castlebar, Co. Mayo, and had an extensive farm there. His house was a well-built, old-fashioned one: it consisted of a basement, containing kitchen and usual offices; a ground floor, entered by the hall-door, containing dining-room, drawing-room, and as well an apartment which was known as the playroom; while on the floor above this were the bedrooms, the door of mine being just beside the head of a staircase.

"When I arrived the men who were engaged in working on the farm told me that the house was haunted. I paid no attention to them, as I thought they were only trying to have a joke with a new hand. However, I speedily changed my opinion! One day, shortly after my arrival, I was sitting in the dining-room talking to Mr. B., when the hall door bell rang violently. I got up to open the door and admit the visitor, but Mr. B. motioned me to sit down. The housekeeper came running up from the basement, to know if her master had rung for her. He replied that he had not, and when she had left the room he turned to me and said, 'There's the ghost!' Then he told me that this ringing was of frequent occurrence, and that footsteps were heard about the house—in the hall, on the stairs, and especially in that room known as the 'playroom'; though nothing seems ever to have been heard in the basement.

"From my own experience I found that what he had told me was the case. When I was in bed I frequently heard heavy footsteps coming slowly up the stairs to the top landing, passing the door of my room, and then apparently turning and going downstairs again. Once, and once only (I am thankful to say!) I had a still more unpleasant experience. I was in bed, and the room was in darkness. I heard the now familiar footsteps coming up the stairs, but instead of turning and descending again, the door opened and the steps came slowly into my room and advanced towards my bed. I could see nothing, but I *felt* as if some unearthly presence were bending over the bed and closely scrutinising me. I always slept with a flash-lamp under my pillow, and although I was terrified I had the presence of mind to pull out the lamp and flash on the light. As was to be expected, I saw nothing. After that experience I always had one of Mr. B.'s sons sleeping in the room with me.

"On several other occasions I heard ringing of bells which could not be accounted for by human agency. I also heard noises, especially in the dining-room and playroom; sometimes these sounded like footsteps, at other times as if someone were lifting up the fender a little and letting it drop again. These and similar noises were heard by many people over a number of years. Before Mr. B. came into possession of the house it was owned by Mr. S. The noises were then heard, and Mr. S., who was a Roman Catholic, got a priest in to say Mass, but to no avail. Mr. B. has died, and since I returned home I had a letter from his brother, who said that for the last couple of years no noises have been heard."

A house in the North of Ireland, near that locality which is eternally famous as having furnished the material for the last trial for witchcraft in the country, is said to be haunted, the reason being that it is built on the site of a disused and very ancient graveyard. It is said that when some repairs were being carried out nine human skulls were unearthed. It would be interesting to ascertain how many houses in Ireland are traditionally said to be built on such unpleasant sites, and if they all bear the reputation of being haunted. The present writer knows of one, in the South, which is so situated (and this is supported, to a certain extent, by documentary evidence from the thirteenth century down) and which in consequence has an uncanny reputation. But concerning the above house it has been found almost impossible to get any information. It is said that strange noises were frequently heard there, which sometimes seemed as if cartloads of stones were being run down one of the gables. On one occasion an inmate of the house lay dying upstairs. A friend went up to see the sick person, and on proceeding to pass through the bedroom door was pressed and jostled as if by some unseen person hurriedly leaving the room. On entering, it was found that the sick person had just passed away.

Half-way up the Clogher Valley, in the townland of Cavnakirk, once stood a small house, now levelled to the ground, in and around which the following incidents occurred.[5] At the time the house was occupied by a brother and sister named Wilson, who farmed some acres of mountain-land; a younger brother, a scapegrace, had emigrated to Canada, and it was well known that previous to his departure he had lived on very bad terms with his sister.

One summer evening George Wilson had returned home from his work, driving the cows before him, and after tying them in the byre, he had gone into the kitchen and sat down to his supper. As he crossed the yard he met his sister on her way out to milk. The sun had set, but as he sat by the window in the bright summer twilight he could see his sister as she sat milking just inside the byre door. She was singing, and he could hear the hiss of the milk as it steamed into the pail; then for a moment he dropped his eyes, and as he raised them again he thought he saw a shadowy figure flit across the yard. Suddenly he heard a scream from his

---

[5] *Occult Review*, vol. viii. p.19.

sister—he started up and rushed out, and as he crossed the yard he could hear her struggling and panting, like one fighting for life. On reaching the byre door he found her half-standing, half-lying against the wall, her face black and her eyes starting from her head, while her two hands were tearing at her throat as if trying to break the grip of some invisible assailant. At her brother's entrance the pressure seemed to relax; she was too far gone to speak, but he carried her back to the house, where nearly an hour passed before she was able to give a coherent account of what had happened.

Briefly her story was as follows: while engaged in milking she had looked up, and saw her brother, who had gone to Canada, turn the corner of the house. Her first thought naturally was that he had returned home, but the next moment the figure, now grown dim and shadowy, rushed at her, and seizing her by the throat, tried to strangle her. She could feel his grip, and see his shadowy arms, but struggle as she could her hands encountered no solid substance, yet strangled she would have been had not her other brother rushed in. When he entered, the shadowy form loosed its hold and glided away round the corner, but ere it vanished it turned a malignant look on her, and she was positive it was the face of her absent brother.

She was in a state of collapse, and refused to go to bed, so brother and sister sat by the fire until break of day. With the dawn her fears abated, and she consented to lie down, but she insisted that her brother should bring his bed into her room and sleep there.

That evening they went early to bed, but night had hardly fallen ere a terrible racket started in the kitchen. George Wilson rose and lit a candle, and instantly the noise ceased, but no sooner had he returned to his bed than the strange sounds began again;

and so it continued through the entire night. Thoroughly alarmed by this, they told some of their neighbours, and two or three of them volunteered to keep them company on the following night. They sat in the kitchen and everything was perfectly quiet. Then Wilson suggested that they should extinguish the light and retire to the room. Hardly had they done this than a terrific crash sounded in the kitchen, as if all the pewter and delft ware on the dresser had been flung to the ground. Candle in hand, one of the visitors sprang into the kitchen, but there was no sign of any disturbance there. In vain the company searched, but there was no sign of anything unusual; they had hardly resumed their places in the room when there came a crash against the wall as if a chair had been flung violently across the kitchen. Renewed search was useless, and so the night passed, until the break of day put an end to the disturbance.

Night after night these noises continued, until the unfortunate Wilsons were driven almost insane with fright, and could get no sleep unless they went to a neighbour's house. Finally they enlisted the services of a man named Richard Robinson, who was deeply religious, and had the reputation of being absolutely fearless where ghosts were concerned. He spent a night in the bedroom with the brother and sister, making them lie down on their beds, while he sat on a chair, and kept the candle lighted. For a time everything was quiet. Then there came a sudden crash and a moment later a chair was upset. Then a scream from the girl attracted him, and he saw that her bed was heaving as if someone beneath it was pressing upwards. He cut underneath it with a sword he had brought, and immediately the movement ceased; but a chair at the opposite side of the room was flung down. After another movement of the bed a sound was heard as if the tongs were flung violently across the kitchen. Robinson rushed out, to find the place empty, but was hastily brought back again by a scream from the girl. He found her in a state of abject terror, declaring that a shadowy figure had leaped on the bed, and made as if it would have gripped her by the throat. He brother saw nothing, but felt the pressure on the bed. Life became unbearable for the two Wilsons, so in the autumn they sold their farm and emigrated—to America, it is believed. Before they left their home they learnt that their brother in Canada had met his death—how was not certainly known, as the letter conveying the intelligence was couched in very vague language—on the very day that his shadowy form had assailed his sister.

An account of a most unpleasant haunting is contributed by Mr. W. S. Thompson, who vouches for the substantial accuracy of it, and also furnishes the names of two men still living, who attended the "station." We give it as it stands, with the comment that some of the details seem to have been grossly exaggerated by local raconteurs. In the year 1869 a ghost made its presence manifest in the house of a Mr. M— in Co. Cavan. In the daytime it resided in the chimney, but at night it left its quarters and subjected the family to considerable annoyance. During the day they could cook nothing, as showers of soot would be sent down the chimney on top of every pot and pan that was placed on the fire. At night the various members of the family would be dragged out of bed by the hair, and pulled around the house. When anyone ventured to light a lamp it would immediately be put out, while chairs and tables would be sent dancing round the room. At last matters reached such a pitch that the family found it impossible to remain any longer in the house. The night before they left Mrs. M— was severely handled, and her boots left facing the door as a gentle hint for her to be off. Before they departed some of the neighbours went to the house, saw the ghost, and even described to Mr. Thompson what they had seen. According to one man it appeared in the shape of a human being with a pig's head with long tusks. Another described it as a horse with an elephant's head, and a headless man seated on its back. Finally a "station" was held at the house by seven priests, at which all the neighbours attended. The station commenced after sunset, and everything in the house had to be uncovered, lest the evil spirit should find any resting-place. A free passage was left out of the door into the street, where many people were kneeling. About five minutes after the station opened a rumbling noise was heard, and a black barrel rolled out with an unearthly din, though to some coming up the street it appeared in the shape of a black horse with a bull's head, and a headless man seated thereon. From this time the ghost gave no further trouble.

The same gentleman also sends an account of a haunted shop in which members of his family had some very unpleasant experiences. "In October 1882 my father, William Thompson, took over the grocery and spirit business from a Dr. S— to whom it had been left by will. My sister was put in charge of the business, and she slept on the premises at night, but she was not there by herself very long until she found things amiss. The third night matters were made so unpleasant for her that she had to get up out of bed more dead than alive, and go across the street to Mrs. M—, the servant at the R.I.C. barrack, with whom she remained until the morning. She stated that as she lay in bed, half awake and half asleep, she saw a man enter the room, who immediately seized her by the throat and well-nigh choked her. She had only sufficient strength left to gasp 'Lord, save me!' when instantly the man vanished. She also said that she heard noises as if every bottle and glass in the shop was smashed to atoms, yet in the morning everything would be found intact. My brother was in charge of the shop one day, as my sister had to go to Belturbet to do some Christmas shopping. He expected her to return to the shop that night, but as she did not do so he was preparing to go to bed about 1 A.M., when suddenly a terrible noise was heard. The light was extinguished, and the tables and chairs commenced to dance about the floor, and some of them struck him on the shins. Upon this he left the house, declaring that he had seen the Devil!" Possibly this ghost had been a rabid teetotaller in the flesh, and continued to have a dislike to the publican's trade after he had become discarnate. At any rate the present occupants, who follow a different avocation, do not appear to be troubled.

Ghosts are no respecters of persons or places, and take up their quarters where they are least expected. One can hardly imagine them entering a R.I.C. barrack, and annoying the stalwart inmates thereof. Yet more than one tale of a haunted police-barrack has been sent to us—nay, in its proper place we shall relate the appearance of a deceased member of the "Force," uniform and all! The following personal experiences are contributed by an ex-R.I.C. constable, who requested that all names should be suppressed. "The barrack of which I am about to speak has now disappeared, owing to the construction of a new railway line. It was a three-storey house, with large airy apartments and splendid accommodation. This particular night I was on guard. After the constables had retired to their quarters I took my palliasse downstairs to the day-room, and laid it on two forms alongside two six-foot tables which were placed end to end in the centre of the room.

"As I expected a patrol in at midnight, and as another had to be sent out when it arrived, I didn't promise myself a very restful night, so I threw myself on the bed, intending to read a bit, as there was a large lamp on the table. Scarcely had I commenced to read when I felt as if I was being pushed off the bed. At first I thought I must have fallen asleep, so to make sure, I got up, took a few turns around the room, and then deliberately lay down again and took up my book. Scarcely had I done so, when the same thing happened, and, though I resisted with all my strength, I was finally landed on the floor. My bed was close to the table, and the pushing came from that side, so that if anyone was playing a trick on me they could not do so without being under the table: I looked, but there was no visible presence there. I felt shaky, but changed my couch to another part of the room, and had no further unpleasant experience. Many times after I was 'guard' in the same room, but I always took care not to place my couch in that particular spot.

"One night, long afterwards, we were all asleep in the dormitory, when we were awakened in the small hours of the morning by the guard rushing upstairs, dashing through the room, and jumping into a bed in the farthest corner behind its occupant. There he lay gasping, unable to speak for several minutes, and even then we couldn't get a coherent account of what befel him. It appears he fell asleep, and suddenly awoke to find himself on the floor, and a body rolling over him. Several men volunteered to go downstairs with him, but he absolutely refused to leave the dormitory, and stayed there till morning. Nor would he even remain downstairs at night without having a comrade with him. It ended in his applying for an exchange of stations.

"Another time I returned off duty at midnight, and after my comrade, a married Sergeant, had gone outside to his quarters I went to the kitchen to change my boots. There was a good fire on, and it looked so comfortable that I remained toasting my toes on the hob, and enjoying my pipe. The lock-up was a lean-to one-storey building off the kitchen, and was divided into two cells, one opening into the kitchen, the other into that cell. I was smoking away quietly when I suddenly heard inside the lock-up a dull, heavy thud, just like the noise a drunken man would make by crashing down on all-fours. I wondered who the prisoner could be, as I didn't see anyone that night who seemed a likely candidate for free lodgings. However as I heard no other sound I decided I would tell the guard in order that he might look after him. As I took my candle from the table I happened to glance at the lock-up, and, to my surprise, I saw that the outer door was open. My curiosity being roused, I looked inside, to find the inner door also open. There was nothing in either cell, except the two empty plank-beds, and these were immovable as they were firmly fixed to the walls. I betook myself to my bedroom much quicker than I was in the habit of doing.

"I mentioned that this barrack was demolished owing to the construction of a new railway line. It was the last obstacle removed, and in the meantime workmen came from all points of the compass. One day a powerful navvy was brought into the barrack a total collapse from drink, and absolutely helpless. After his neckwear was loosened he was carried to the lock-up and laid on the plank-bed, the guard being instructed to visit him periodically, lest he should smother. He was scarcely half an hour there—this was in the early evening—when the most unmerciful screaming brought all hands to the lock-up, to find the erstwhile helpless man standing on the plank-bed, and grappling with a, to us, invisible foe. We took him out, and he maintained that a man had tried to choke him, and was still there when we came to his relief. The strange thing was, that he was shivering with fright, and perfectly sober, though in the ordinary course of events he would not be in that condition for at least seven or eight hours. The story spread like wildfire through the town, but the inhabitants were not in the least surprised, and one old man told us that many strange things happened in that house long before it became a police-barrack."

A lady, who requests that her name be suppressed, relates a strange sight seen by her sister in Galway. The latter's husband was stationed in that town about seventeen years ago. One afternoon he was out, and she was lying on a sofa in the drawing-room, when suddenly from behind a screen (where there was no door) came a little old woman, with a small shawl over her head and shoulders, such as the country women used to wear. She had a most diabolical expression on her face. She seized the lady by the hand, and said: "I will drag you down to Hell, where I am!" The lady sprang up in terror and shook her off, when the horrible creature again disappeared behind the screen. The house was an old one, and many stories were rife amongst the people about it, the one most to the point being that the apparition of an old woman, who was supposed to have poisoned someone, used to be seen therein. Needless to say, the lady in question never again sat by herself in the drawing-room.

Two stories are told about haunted houses at Drogheda, the one by A. G. Bradley in *Notes on some Irish Superstitions* (Drogheda, 1894), the other by F. G. Lee in *Sights and Shadows* (p. 42). As both appear to be placed at the same date, *i.e.* 1890, it is quite possible that they refer to one and the same haunting, and we have so treated them accordingly. The reader, if he wishes, can test the matter for himself.

This house, which was reputed to be haunted, was let to a tailor and his wife by the owner at an annual rent of £23. They took possession in due course, but after a very few days they became aware of the presence of a most unpleasant supernatural lodger. One night, as the tailor and his wife were preparing to retire, they were terrified at seeing the foot of some invisible person kick the candlestick off the table, and so quench the candle. Although it was a very dark night, and the shutters were closed, the man and his wife could see everything in the room just as well as if it were the middle of the day. All at once a woman entered the room, dressed in white, carrying something in her hand, which she threw at the tailor's wife, striking her with some violence, and then vanished. While this was taking place on the first floor, a most frightful noise was going on overhead in the room where the children and their nurse were sleeping. The father immediately rushed upstairs, and found to his horror the floor all torn up, the furniture broken, and, worst of all, the children lying senseless and naked on the bed, and having the appearance of having been severely beaten. As he was leaving the room with the children in his arms he suddenly remembered that he had not seen the nurse, so he turned back with the intention of bringing her downstairs, but could find her nowhere. The girl, half-dead with fright, and very much bruised, had fled to her mother's house, where she died in a few days in agony.

Because of these occurrences they were legally advised to refuse to pay any rent. The landlady, however, declining to release them from their bargain, at once claimed a quarter's rent; and when this remained for some time unpaid, sued them for it before Judge Kisby. A Drogheda solicitor appeared for the tenants, who, having given evidence of the facts concerning the ghost in question, asked leave to support their sworn testimony by that of several other people. This, however, was disallowed by the judge. It was admitted by the landlady that nothing on one side or the other had been said regarding the haunting when the house was let. A judgment was consequently entered for the landlady, although it had been shown indirectly that unquestionably the house had

had the reputation of being haunted, and that previous tenants had been much inconvenienced.

This chapter may be concluded with two stories dealing with haunted rectories. The first of these was published at second-hand in the previous edition of this book, but we are now enabled to give it direct from the manuscript of the principal percipient, a well-known Canon (since retired) in the Diocese of Clogher. He writes as follows:

"On Christmas Eve 1885, my attention was directed by my cook to a curious noise, somewhat like what a very heavily-laden wagon passing close to a rather rickety house would make. At first I gave but little heed to her alarm; to be quite candid, I suspected the presence of a tipsy sweetheart, and it being the Festive Season I did *not* want to know everything. However, the woman's manner betokened sincerity and genuine fear of something, so I called my man-servant, and we descended, a dauntless three, to the kitchen. Arrived there we found the vibrating noise to increase strongly, and the whole basement of the house to be in a condition suggestive of the working of an earthquake, but without any of the furniture or dishes being moved or in any way disturbed. Two brilliant lamps, one on the wall, and the other on the table in the middle of the rather small kitchen, afforded light almost as clear as daylight. We three stood in amazement at what was, without any visible cause, going on around us, the servants literally clinging to me, one on either side.

"The noise suddenly ceased, both as regards our immediate vicinity and its hitherto rumbling character, while a pantry right in front of which we stood became the scene of fresh disturbances. There it seemed as if china, dishes, and glass were being thrown with tremendous violence on the flagged floor. As soon as each crash resounded in our ears the terrified domestics clung with intense fervour to my arms. Convinced now of the fact that some 'game' was being played on me, of which my servants were the sharers, if not the actual devisers, I resolved to open the pantry door, which was locked but had the key in it, and investigate the mystery, if such it should prove to be. But my suggestion simply threw my panic-stricken companions almost into fits, and they implored me not to do so. I replied to them: 'Yes, in God's name I *will* open the door, and if you two are too cowardly to follow me, I shall go in by myself, and discover the secret of all the confusion.' Accordingly I made a quick and very energetic movement towards the scene of the mysterious noise, *when slowly the locked door of the pantry opened,* and out glided a tall female figure, dressed in a loose white dress, with a short black cape round her shoulders. I was literally paralysed with fright. My now almost frantic servants gripped me by each arm as in a vice, causing me intense pain, and, as it subsequently turned out, leaving the marks of their grips for many days in the fleshy part of my arms. It was to this sharp physical pain I attribute the passing away of the feeling of faintness caused by the apparition, and the restoration to a state of comparative coolness.

"I rushed after the figure, which continued to move towards the stairs, which as soon as she had reached she vanished from sight. Scarcely had she done so when my two little boys at the top of the house, three storeys higher than where I stood, screamed out, 'There is a woman in white in the room with us.' I literally fled up to the boys' room, followed by my two sharers of the vision. On arriving there I closely questioned the children. The eldest, aged ten, told me he had lain awake to watch for Santa Claus, but instead of the genial old Children's Friend he saw a strange lady, who just glided into the room and out again, leaving no toys, no any other trace of her presence. Every place was searched without avail, but no token of our strange visitor was found. The pantry door was *still locked*, and on its being opened no sign of anything having been disturbed was discoverable.

"Since then the same visitant has been seen by myself, by other members of the family, and by visitors. Nothing dreadful has been observed as happening in connection with her visits. I have selected the above instance of these appearances because (1) it was the first time anyone would admit that they had seen anything; (2) because I myself was a principal witness of it; (3) because it was seen by at least four persons—my two servants, my ten-year-old boy, and myself at practically the same moment. At other times some of us have seen it alone. I do not pretend to explain anything about these appearances, but solemnly do I declare that all I have said is a plain unvarnished tale of facts within my own experience."

The second of these, which is decidedly more complex and mystifying, refers to a rectory in Co. Donegal. It is sent as the personal experience of one of the percipients, who does not wish to have his name disclosed. He says: "My wife, children, and myself will have lived here four years next January (1914). From the first night that we came into the house most extraordinary noises have been heard. Sometimes they were inside the house, and seemed as if the furniture was being disturbed, and the fire-irons knocked about, or at other times as if a dog was running up and down stairs. Sometimes they were external, and resembled tin buckets being dashed about the yard, or as if a herd of cattle was galloping up the drive before the windows. These things would go on for six months, and then everything would be quiet for three months or so, when the noises would commence again. My dogs—a fox-terrier, a boar-hound, and a spaniel—would make a terrible din, and would bark at something in the hall we could not see, backing away from it all the time.

"The only thing that was ever *seen* was as follows: one night my daughter went down to the kitchen about ten o'clock for some hot water. She saw a tall man, with one arm, carrying a lamp, who walked out of the pantry into the kitchen, and then through the kitchen wall. Another daughter saw the same man walk down one evening from the loft, and go into the harness-room. She told me, and I went out immediately, but could see nobody. Shortly after that my wife, who is very brave, heard a knock at the hall door in the dusk. Naturally thinking it was some friend, she opened the door, and there saw standing outside the self-same man. He simply looked at her, and walked through the wall into the house. She got such a shock that she could not speak for several hours, and was ill for some days. That is eighteen months ago, and he has not been seen since, and it is six months since we heard any noises." Our correspondent's letter was written on 25th November 1913. "An old man nearly ninety died last year. He lived all his life within four hundred yards of this house, and used to tell me that seventy years ago the parsons came with bell, book, and candle to drive the ghosts out of the house." Evidently they were unsuccessful. In English ghost stories it is the parson who performs the exorcism successfully, while in Ireland such work is generally performed by the priest. Indeed a tale was sent to us in which a ghost quite ignored the parson's efforts, but succumbed to the priest.

III

HAUNTED HOUSES IN MOGH'S HALF

THE northern half of Ireland has not proved as prolific in stories of haunted houses as the southern portion; the possible explanation of this is, not that the men of the north are less prone to hold, or talk about, such beliefs, but that, as regards the south half, we have had the good fortune to happen upon some diligent collectors of these and kindred tales, whose eagerness in collecting is only equalled by their kindness in imparting information to the compilers of this book.

On a large farm near Portarlington there once lived a Mrs.——, a strong-minded, capable woman, who managed all her affairs for herself, giving her orders, and taking none from anybody. In due time she died, and the property passed to the next-of-kin. As soon, however, as the funeral was over, the house was nightly disturbed by strange noises: people downstairs would hear rushings about in the upper rooms, banging of doors, and the sound of heavy footsteps. The cups and saucers used to fall off the dresser, and all the pots and pans would rattle.

This went on for some time, till the people could stand it no longer, so they left the house and put in a herd and his family. The latter was driven away after he had been in the house a few weeks. This happened to several people, until at length a man named Mr. B— took the house. The noises went on as before until someone suggested getting the priest in. Accordingly the priest came, and held a service in the late Mrs. ——'s bedroom. When this was over, the door of the room was locked. After that the noises were not heard till one evening Mr. B— came home from a fair, fortified, no doubt, with a little "Dutch courage," and declared that even if the devil were in it he would go into the locked room. In spite of all his family could say or do, he burst open the door, and entered the room, but apparently saw nothing. That night pandemonium reigned in the house, the chairs were hurled about, the china was broken, and the most weird and uncanny sounds were heard. Next day the priest was sent for, the room again shut up, and nothing has happened from that day to this.

Another strange story comes from the same town. "When I was on a visit to a friend in Portarlington," writes a lady in the *Journal of the American S.P.R.*[6] "a rather unpleasant incident occurred to me. At about two o'clock in the morning I woke up suddenly, for apparently no reason whatever; however, I quite distinctly heard snoring coming from under or in the bed in which I was lying. It continued for about ten minutes, during which time I was absolutely limp with fright. The door opened, and my friend entered the bedroom, saying, 'I thought you might want me, so I came in.' Needless to say, I hailed the happy inspiration that sent her to me. I then told her what I had heard; she listened to me, and then to comfort (!) me said, 'Oh, never mind; *it is only grandfather!* He died in this room, and a snoring

---

[6]   For September 1913.

is heard every night at two o'clock, the hour at which he passed away.' Some time previously a German gentleman was staying with this family. They asked him in the morning how he had slept, and he replied that he was disturbed by a snoring in the room, but he supposed it was the cat."

A lady, formerly resident in Queen's Co., but who now lives near Dublin, sends the following clear and concise account of her own personal experiences in a haunted house: "Some years ago, my father, mother, sister, and myself went to live in a nice but rather small-house close to the town of —— in Queen's Co. We liked the house, as it was conveniently and pleasantly situated, and we certainly never had a thought of ghosts or haunted houses, nor would my father allow any talk about such things in his presence. But we were not long settled there when we were disturbed by the opening of the parlour door every night regularly at the hour of eleven o'clock. My father and mother used to retire to their room about ten o'clock, while my sister and I used to sit up reading. We always declared that we would retire before the door opened, but we generally got so interested in our books that we would forget until we would hear the handle of the door turn, and see the door flung open. We tried in every way to account for this, but we could find no explanation, and there was no possibility of any human agent being at work.

"Some time after, light was thrown on the subject. We had visitors staying with us, and in order to make room for them, my sister was asked to sleep in the parlour. She consented without a thought of ghosts, and went to sleep quite happily; but during the night she was awakened by someone opening the door, walking across the room, and disturbing the fireirons. She, supposing it to be the servant, called her by name, but got no answer: then the person seemed to come away from the fireplace, and walk out of the room. There was a fire in the grate, but though she heard the footsteps, she could see no one.

"The next thing was, that I was coming downstairs, and as I glanced towards the hall door I saw standing by it a man in a grey suit. I went to my father and told him. He asked in surprise who let him in, as the servant was out, and he himself had already locked, bolted, and chained the door an hour previously. None of us had let him in, and when my father went out to the hall the man had disappeared, and the door was as he had left it.

"Some little time after, I had a visit from a lady who knew the place well, and in the course of conversation she said:

"'This is the house poor Mr. —— used to live in.'

"'Who is Mr. ——?' I asked.

"'Did you never hear of him?' she replied. 'He was a minister who used to live in this house quite alone, and was murdered in this very parlour. His landlord used to visit him sometimes, and one night he was seen coming in about eleven o'clock, and was seen again leaving about five o'clock in the morning. When Mr. —— did not come out as usual, the door was forced open, and he was found lying dead in this room by the fender, with his head battered in with the poker.'

"We left the house soon after," adds our informant.

The following weird incidents occurred, apparently in the Co. Kilkenny, to a Miss K. B., during two visits paid by her to Ireland in 1880 and 1881. The house in which she experienced the following was really an old barrack, long disused, very old-fashioned, and surrounded with a high wall; it was said that it had been built during the time of Cromwell as a stronghold for his men. The only inhabitants of this were Captain C— (a retired officer in charge of the place), Mrs. C—, three daughters, and two servants. They occupied the central part of the building, the mess-room being their drawing-room. Miss K. B.'s bedroom was very lofty, and adjoined two others which were occupied by the three daughters, E., G., and L.

"The first recollection I have of anything strange," writes Miss B., "was that each night I was awakened about three o'clock by a tremendous noise, apparently in the next suite of rooms, which was empty, and it sounded as if some huge iron boxes and other heavy things were being thrown about with great force. This continued for about half an hour, when in the room underneath (the kitchen) I heard the fire being violently poked and raked for several minutes, and this was immediately followed by a most terrible and distressing cough of a man, very loud and violent. It seemed as if the exertion had brought on a paroxysm which he could not stop. In large houses in Co. Kilkenny the fires are not lighted every day, owing to the slow-burning property of the coal, and it is only necessary to rake it up every night about eleven o'clock, and in the morning it is still bright and clear. Consequently I wondered why it was necessary for Captain C— to get up in the middle of the night to stir it so violently."

A few days later Miss B. said to E. C.: "I hear such strange noises every night—are there any people in the adjoining part of the building?" She turned very pale, and looking earnestly at Miss B., said, "Oh K., I am so sorry you heard. I hoped no one but myself had heard it. I could have given worlds to have spoken to you last night, but dared not move or speak." K. B. laughed at her for being so superstitious, but E. declared that the place was haunted, and told her of a number of weird things that had been seen and heard.

In the following year, 1881, Miss K. B. paid another visit to the barrack. This time there were two other visitors there—a colonel and his wife. They occupied Miss B.'s former room, while to her was allotted a huge bedroom on the top of the house, with a long corridor leading to it; opposite to this was another large room, which was occupied by the girls.

Her strange experiences commenced again. "One morning, about four o'clock, I was awakened by a very noisy martial footstep ascending the stairs, and then marching quickly up and down the corridor outside my room. Then suddenly the most violent coughing took place that I ever heard, which continued for some time, while the quick, heavy step continued its march. At last the footsteps faded away in the distance, and I then recalled to mind the same coughing after exertion last year." In the morning, at breakfast, she asked both Captain C— and the colonel had they been walking about, but both denied, and also said they had no cough. The family looked very uncomfortable, and afterwards E. came up with tears in her eyes, and said, "Oh K., please don't say anything more about that dreadful coughing; we all hear it often, especially when anything terrible is about to happen."

Some nights later the C—s gave a dance. When the guests had departed, Miss B. went to her bedroom. "The moon was shining so beautifully that I was able to read my Bible by its light, and had left the Bible open on the window-sill, which was a very high one, and on which I sat to read, having had to climb the washstand to reach it. I went to bed, and fell asleep, but was not long so when I was suddenly awakened by the strange feeling that someone was in the room. I opened my eyes, and turned around, and saw on the window-sill in the moonlight a long, very thin, very dark figure bending over the Bible, and apparently earnestly scanning the page. As if my movement disturbed the figure, it suddenly darted up, jumped off the window-ledge on to the washstand, then to the ground, and flitted quietly across the room to the table where my jewellery was." That was the last she saw of it. She thought it was someone trying to steal her jewellery, so waited till morning, but nothing was missing. In the morning she described to one of the daughters, G., what she had seen, and the latter told her that something always happened when that appeared. Miss K. B. adds that nothing did happen. Later on she was told that a colonel had cut his throat in that very room.

Another military station, Charles Fort, near Kinsale, has long had the reputation of being haunted. An account of this was sent to the *Wide World Magazine* (Jan. 1908), by Major H. L. Ruck Keene, D.S.O.; he states that he took it from a manuscript written by a Captain Marvell Hull about the year 1880. Further information on the subject of the haunting is to be found in Dr. Craig's *Real Pictures of Clerical Life in Ireland*.

Charles Fort was erected in 1667 by the Duke of Ormonde. It is said to be haunted by a ghost known as the "White Lady," and the traditional account of the reason for this haunting is briefly as follows: shortly after the erection of the fort, a Colonel Warrender, a severe disciplinarian, was appointed its governor. He had a daughter, who bore the quaint Christian name of "Wilful"; she became engaged to a Sir Trevor Ashurst, and subsequently married him. On the evening of their wedding-day the bride and bridegroom were walking on the battlements, when she espied some flowers growing on the rocks beneath. She expressed a wish for them, and a sentry posted close by volunteered to climb down for them, provided Sir Trevor took his place during his absence. He assented, and took the soldier's coat and musket while he went in search of a rope. Having obtained one, he commenced his descent; but the task proving longer than he expected, Sir Trevor fell asleep. Meantime the governor visited the sentries, as was his custom, and in the course of his rounds came to where Sir Trevor was asleep. He challenged him, and on receiving no answer perceived that he was asleep, whereupon he drew a pistol and shot him through the heart. The body was brought in, and it was only then the governor realised what had happened. The bride, who appears to have gone indoors before the tragedy occurred, then learned the fate that befell her husband, and in her distraction, rushed from the house and flung herself over the battlements. In despair at the double tragedy, her father shot himself during the night.

The above is from Dr. Craig's book already alluded to. In the *Wide World Magazine* the legend differs slightly in details. According to this the governor's name was Browne, and it was his own son, not his son-in-law, that he shot; while the incident is said to have occurred about a hundred and fifty years ago.

The "White Lady" is the ghost of the young bride. Let us see what accounts there are of her appearance. A good many years ago Fort-Major Black, who had served in the Peninsular War, gave his own personal experience to Dr. Craig. He stated that he had gone to the hall door one summer evening, and saw a lady entering the door and going up the stairs. At first he thought she was an officer's wife, but as he looked, he observed she was dressed in white, and in a very old-fashioned style. Impelled by curiosity, he hastened upstairs after her, and followed her closely into one of the rooms, but on entering it he could not find the slightest trace of anyone there. On another occasion he stated that two sergeants were packing some cast stores. One of them had his little daughter with him, and the child suddenly exclaimed, "Who is that white lady who is bending over the banisters, and looking down at us?" The two men looked up, but could see nothing, but the child insisted that she had seen a lady in white looking down and smiling at her.

On another occasion a staff officer, a married man, was residing in the "Governor's House." One night as the nurse lay awake— she and the children were in a room which opened into what was known as the White Lady's apartment—she suddenly saw a lady clothed in white glide to the bedside of the youngest child, and after a little place her hand upon its wrist. At this the child started in its sleep, and cried out, "Oh! Take that cold hand from my wrist!" The next moment the lady disappeared.

One night, about the year 1880, Captain Marvell Hull and Lieutenant Hartland were going to the rooms occupied by the former officer. As they reached a small landing they saw distinctly in front of them a woman in a white dress. As they stood there in awestruck silence she turned and looked towards them, showing a face beautiful enough, but colourless as a corpse, and then passed on through a locked door.

But it appears that this presence did not always manifest itself in as harmless a manner. Some years ago Surgeon L— was quartered at the fort. One day he had been out snipe-shooting, and as he entered the fort the mess-bugle rang out. He hastened to his rooms to dress, but as he failed to put in an appearance at mess, one of the officers went in search of him, and found him lying senseless on the floor. When he recovered consciousness he related his experience. He said he had stooped down for the key of his door, which he had placed for safety under the mat; when in this position he felt himself violently dragged across the hall, and flung down a flight of steps. With this agrees somewhat the experience of a Captain Jarves, as related by him to Captain Marvell Hull. Attracted by a strange rattling noise in his bedroom, he endeavoured to open the door of it, but found it seemingly locked. Suspecting a hoax, he called out, whereupon a gust of wind passed him, and some unseen power flung him down the stairs, and laid him senseless at the bottom.

A lady, Miss Dorothy Emerson, contributes the following account of hauntings in Co. Cork:

"Three times in my life I have lived in haunted houses. I was born in the first, and we left it when I was about three years old, so I myself have no recollection of anything that took place, but I certainly saw something there, for my mother has often told me the story since. It appears that one day she was sitting in the drawing-room and I was playing about. She asked me to go upstairs with a message for my nurse, so off I started, but came back in a few seconds and told her I couldn't go upstairs, as I didn't like to pass the lady in the hall. Thinking that somebody must have got into the house without being noticed, she went out, taking me with her. To her astonishment there was no one there, so she asked me where I had seen the lady. I pointed to a large ottoman that stood at the foot of the stairs and said, 'The lady is there!' Mother thought it was all nonsense on my part, so she took me by the hand and started for the stairs, but pass the ottoman I would not. I took a firm stand and said, 'I won't go past the lady!' I did not make a fuss, but she could not make me go past. She herself saw absolutely nothing, but she could see that I did, so she wisely did not force me. She said nothing about the occurrence to anyone, but a short time after, my nurse saw the very self-same lady in black sitting on the ottoman.

"The next house we lived in was a large country-house standing in about fifty acres of land, called 'Melton.' On the whole, this house was singularly quiet, except for one or two occurrences. She I was about five years old two cousins came to stay with us. The eldest, Elizabeth, was a girl about sixteen years old, and the youngest a little older than myself. They slept in a double-bed in the nursery, and I slept beside them on a small stretcher. Before I go any further I should say that Elizabeth was psychical, and had seen many queer things, but never up to this at 'Melton.' One night she woke up about two o'clock with a horrid feeling that someone was standing beside her bed. She saw nothing, but presently she felt a hand touch her. (I forgot to say that the room was lighted, as the door was kept open, and a large lamp stood outside on the landing.) The hand passed up her whole body and over her face, and she lay there absolutely frozen with terror. Just then I woke up, turned round, and sitting bolt upright, cried out, 'Oh, look at the burglar, Elizabeth, he is standing beside you!' Then I started to cry, and she had to shake off her fears and get out and soothe me. The think appeared to vanish because when she got back to bed nothing more happened and she fell asleep. In the morning she told herself that it was all a dream either on her part or on mine, but when my mother came into the room I informed her that there was a nasty man standing beside Elizabeth's bed in the night, and that I was sure it was a burglar, or, as I pronounced it, 'a buggler.' Fearing lest she might frighten me, Elizabeth pretended to me that I had dreamt it, but privately she told my mother what had happened. Certainly something must have been there, because she felt it and I saw it.

"Some years later, when I was about thirteen years old, I was going up to bed one night again with the two cousins before mentioned.

"The landing in front of me was in darkness, and the only light we had was a candle held by Elizabeth. I was going gaily ahead, and we were all three laughing, when suddenly out of the gloom ahead a ghastly white malevolent face appeared; it hung in the gloom exactly as if it were suspended by the hair. I was horror-stricken, and flinging my arm across my eyes to shut out the sight, I bolted back, very nearly hurling my cousin downstairs. When I looked again it was gone, but some time later when I was back in my house-residence at Alexandra College I saw the very same face hanging in the air on a dusky landing on a dark evening about six o'clock, and the appalling wickedness of its expression left me speechless.

"But to go back to 'Melton.' Twice I heard my name called, once when I was helping Janie, the housemaid, to make a bed. The rest of the family had driven off down town, and the cook was out with the fowl. Suddenly a voice called out, 'Dorothy!' We both heard it, because Janie said, 'Why, there's the mistress calling, she must have forgotten something and come back!' So I cried out, 'Yes!' and ran downstairs, but there was not a soul there. Another time a cousin of mine, an English girl, and I were standing near a book-case in the breakfast-room hunting for something. We were absolutely alone in the house, as the servants were hanging out clothes, and everybody else was away. And then a voice called out, 'Adelaide! Dorothy!' and we both cried, 'Yes!' quite involuntarily before we realised that the house was empty. So we rushed out and hunted the house from attic to basement, but couldn't see a soul. Of course, we thought that the servants might be playing tricks, but we found them up in a lane a long way away from the house, and the men were in the kitchen garden.

"This ends my personal experiences at 'Melton,' but two other uncanny things happened there. One night the coachman had driven my cousin, myself, and the servants to a concert some miles away, leaving in the house my father, my mother, and my eldest brother. They were peacefully reading when they were all surprised to hear someone run downstairs into the hall and laugh. Such a devilish, evil laugh! They took a lamp, and going to the hall, searched about, but could see nothing, so they went round the house but found every place locked up and quite peaceful. The last thing that was heard there was rather peculiar. It happened to my mother. It was at night, we youngsters had gone to bed, the servants were out for the evening, and everybody else was assembled in the breakfast-room. Suddenly remembering something she had to do in the kitchen, mother started off to go downstairs. The kitchen was in the basement, and as she opened the door at the head of the stairs she was rather astonished to hear the taps in the sink being turned on and the sound of running water. Thinking the maids must have got in without being heard, she ran downstairs, to find an empty kitchen, and the taps in the sink unturned. Nor was there any sign of running water or leakage anywhere.

"Before leaving the subject of 'Melton,' I must relate what happened to my nurse in the back avenue one evening while she was out chasing a runaway hen. She had an elderly friend, a woman called Dora Shine; this woman was ill, but it was hoped she would get better. My nurse, Mrs. Duke, was not thinking of her at that moment, but she looked up and who should she see walking up the lane in front of her but Dora. 'Oh, she is better, and has come to see me!' said Mrs. Duke to herself and hurried after her. Dora promptly climbed the ditch, and when Mrs. Duke got up to the spot she had vanished. She felt then that something was wrong, and the very next morning she heard that Dora had died just at the time that Mrs. Duke had seen her.

"The third house I lived in was noted for its ghosts. The townspeople would not enter its grounds after nightfall, not even, I do believe, if you offered them money to do so. We ourselves never noticed anything in the grounds, though we knew persons who had. Many people think that a house had to be exceedingly old to be haunted, but in this case that theory certainly did not hold good. First of all, this house was built only about seventy years ago, and the builders of it died within the last twenty-six years. They had been a rich childless couple, absolutely devoted to the house and garden, so much so that I heard that they said that they would never leave it after death. Several people declared that they had met them walking round the paths just as they used to in life. However, as I said, we never saw anything in the grounds, but the most weird things went on in the house. Besides the old couple, or rather the woman, as he was never seen, a drowned child had once been brought into the house. There was a stream in the garden which was very rapid when in flood, and this small child had been swept down, and had been taken into the house and had died there. The child must have also haunted it, as the patter of tiny feet was constantly heard.

"One Sunday evening I was sitting alone in the drawing-room with a big Irish terrier and a black cat. There had been several people in to supper, but at the moment the men were all in the smoking-room and the women upstairs. I could hear them talking faintly , but otherwise everything was very silent. By and by I heard a faint noise in the hall—which was tiled—the noise of footsteps—a child's footsteps. They made that slight pattering noise that one always associates with those flat black shoes children used to wear, which strap round the ankle. Up and down—up and down they went ceaselessly. I listened, and suddenly discovered that the animals were listening also, the cat in a mildly interested way, the dog with all his bristles up. He appeared terribly frightened. So I went out into the hall to see what it could be. There was nothing there, and the instant I went out the footsteps ceased. I waited for a few moments and then went back to my chair, which faced the door. The instant I sat down the noise recommenced. Up and down the tiny footsteps went, and the dog quivered and shook. So I went out again, this time hurriedly, but it was no use. Again I saw nothing. The animals meanwhile watched the door, and by the way their moved their

84

heads I could see that they saw something. I walked in and out several times, and finally the noise ceased when the rest of the party came into the room. A short time after this one of the maids, Ellen, told me the story of the drowned child, which I had not known before. When I told her what I had heard, she told me that she, too, had often heard the footsteps.

"For the first few years we lived there I was away most of the time at school, and as I was only at home for short intervals I never noticed anything. The first I heard of the ghosts was one day, when my cousin, Elizabeth (before mentioned), asked me whether I had ever seen anything in the room I slept in. On telling her 'No,' she told me that one night she woke up to see a woman in black standing beside the bed. Thinking that it was my mother, and that someone must be ill, she sat up and asked, 'Is there anything wrong?' Receiving no reply, she struck a match, and was very astonished to find nobody there, and the door tightly closed. This ghost was a tall woman, very stately, and dressed in stiff, black, rustling silk. On inquiry we found that the late lady of the house exactly answered to this description. My mother saw her too, or rather saw and heard her skirts. She was standing on the landing, and hearing a faint rustling she looked up to see black skirts whisking round the corner on to the next landing. One Saturday morning in the summer one of the maids, Maggie, was brushing down the stairs, and chancing to look up she saw a very tall woman, dressed in black, coming out of my room and standing near the door. Not realising for a moment that it was anything out of the common, she looked down again, and then glanced up to behold the lady moving off to the next landing, and again the black skirts whirled round the corner. So she ran downstairs to find all the womenkind out, except mother, who had not been upstairs for a couple of hours.

"This was a frightfully noisy house, especially at night-time, though a great many things happened in the day-time. Many a night I have waked up about one in the morning to hear someone running violently down the back-stairs. All night long there would be banging and rustling and noises of all descriptions, with frequent knockings on the doors. Sometimes for weeks together we would hear nothing, and then they would recommence. September, we noticed, was the worst month. There were, of course, people who pooh-poohed it all, and said the noises were caused by natural agents, rats and mice, etc. Unfortunately for this theory we had no rats, very few mice, and the cat and dog slept out, not to mention the fact that very often everyone in the house got up to investigate. One night we were sure the window had fallen down, but when we went to search, they were all closed and bolted. Another night we thought every bit of china in the house was broken, as there was such a crashing from the direction of the pantries. 'Oh, goodness,' I said, sitting up in bed, 'the cat must have got in! There'll be murder in the morning!' But the morning brought no broken china nor broken anything else, and the cat was found outside as usual.

"The bathroom was over the kitchen and the floor between was composed of single boards, therefore every word that was said in the kitchen could be heard distinctly in the bathroom. One morning I was in my bath when I distinctly heard the maids go out, one to brush out the hall, the other to do some room. They had hardly gone out when I was startled to hear the unmistakable sound of a chair drawn across the tiled floor. Scrambling into a dressing-gown I rushed on out to the landing just as the two maids, Maggie and Ellen, dashed in from the hall. Leaning over the banisters of the back-stairs I called out, 'Did either of you move a chair?' At the same moment they asked each other the same question. I ran downstairs, to find them having a consultation over a chair that was standing out in the middle of the floor, which they had left against the wall only two or three minutes before. What moved that chair? Certainly no human agency. Yet we all three heard the scraping of it, and the chair itself had left its ordinary position. The animals were upstairs with my mother, and no mouse could have done such a thing, unless it was the size of an elephant!

One summer a Mrs. H. from Dublin came to stay with us. She was greatly interested in anything occult, but, at the same time, was not in the least afraid.

"The month was June, and the weather glorious. Mrs. H. woke up one morning to hear a great noise and rustling on the stairs, sounds which she took to be Maggie at her work and wearing a stiff apron. Thinking that it was only about eight o'clock she turned round again and went to sleep. When she woke up the second time she discovered it was only about four o'clock, so that it must have been much earlier when she was awake before. At breakfast she related the whole story, and afterwards told it to Maggie, who astonished by her saying that she, too, had heard the noises. Indeed, she had waked Ellen up and remarked that, 'The fairies were coming for them for sure!' Footsteps had apparently gone by her door. That evening Mrs. H. was upstairs dressing for dinner; the rest of us were in the breakfast-room. By and by she came out of her room and started to descend the stairs. Somebody motioned to me to pull forward a comfortable chair, which I did. The footsteps came as far as the hall and then ceased.

"'Why, what's she doing?' I said and looked out. There was no one there, a fact which I called out. The rest came and looked over my shoulder, and the next thing was the sight of Mrs. H. descending the stairs again, this time in person. Thinking we must have been mistaken we asked her whether she *had* been down before. She answered in the negative.

"Some time before this occurrence I was away for the week-end, and during my absence another thing happened. It was on the Sunday morning about ten-thirty. Ellen had gone to mass, and Maggie was washing up in the kitchen. The family and the animals were in the breakfast-room. Suddenly they all heard Maggie, as they thought, run violently up the back-stairs, across the landing, open the door, and bang it behind her. Remembering that she had intended to give her an order my mother started up to go and call out to her. However, something claimed her attention, and it was several minutes before she was free to go. At the foot of the stairs something prompted her to go and look into the kitchen. She did so. What was her astonishment to see Maggie there calmly washing up. Maggie, for her part, looked nearly as astonished, and her eyes grew round.

"They both exclaimed simultaneously:

"'Why, Maggie, I thought you went upstairs just now!'

"'Why, ma'am, I thought you were upstairs just now!'

"This time they did go upstairs and searched in every corner, but there wasn't a soul to be seen, and certainly no stranger could have got in without their knowing it.

"In a general way it was a very cheerful house to stay in, but now and again it seemed to acquire a gloomy atmosphere. Sometimes for months at a stretch I would sleep in my haunted room and never even think about ghosts, not even when I would be waked up in the early morning by footsteps running violently down the back-stairs. But, on the other hand, sometimes the house would be unbearable. The very air in it had an evil feeling. For a few nights I used to be stiff with terror, and I could feel that my room was full of something nasty. Once or twice people were waked up by a rap at the door, the rapper being always invited in by them, but never accepting the invitation. Several times a child was heard crying in the house—never by the family, curiously enough, though our banshee is a crying child, but always by some visitor or stranger. One night when someone was ill the coachman slept in the house, and he asked Maggie in the morning if there was a child staying in the house, as he had had one crying upstairs in the night. He was greatly perturbed when Maggie said, 'No.' This same Maggie had a young man, a postman, whom she subsequently married. One night he was seeing her home about nine-thirty or so. As they neared the big gates into the yard, he noticed a man leaning against them. He was going to make some remark about it, when he observed that, though apparently looking at the man, she did not seem to see him nor did she make any remark. He said nothing about it until the next day, and then asked her whether she had seen anything. He had guessed rightly, she had not.

"Oh, it was a weird house! I have sat upstairs in my room and listened to one of the family walk upstairs slowly, rattling a bunch of keys in his pocket, and gone out to speak to him, only to find he wasn't there! Two seconds later I had him strolling across the hall, and when I called out he assured me he had not been upstairs for some hours.

"Some people couldn't bear the house, other people loved it. My youngest brother could not stand it for more than a few days at a time. He said it depressed him horribly, and the atmosphere almost hit him in the face!"

Near a seaside town in the south of Ireland a group of small cottages was built by an old lady, in one of which she lived, while she let the others to her relatives. In process of time all the occupants died, the cottages fell into ruin, and were all pulled down (except the one in which the old lady had lived), the materials being used by a farmer to build a large house which he hoped to let to summer visitors. It was shortly afterwards taken for three years by a gentleman for his family. It should be noted that the house had very bare surroundings; there were no trees near, or out-houses where people could be concealed. Soon after the family came to the house they began to hear raps all over it, on doors, windows, and walls; these raps varied in nature, sometimes being like a sledgehammer, loud and dying away, and sometimes quick and sharp, two or three or five in succession; and all heard them. One morning about 4 A.M., the mother heard very loud knocking on the bedroom door; thinking it was the servant wanting to go to early mass, she said, "Come in," but the knocking continued till the father was awakened by it; he got up, searched the house, but could find no one. The servant's door was slightly open, and he saw that she was sound asleep. That morning a telegram came announcing the death of a beloved uncle just about the hour of the knocking. Some time previous to this the mother was in the kitchen, when a loud explosion took place beside her, startling her very much, but no cause for it could be found, nor were any traces left. This coincided with the death of an aunt, wife to the uncle who died later.

One night the mother went to her bedroom. The blind was drawn, and the shutters closed, when suddenly a great crash came, as if a branch was thrown at the window, and there was a sound of broken glass. She opened the shutters with the expectation of finding the window smashed, but there was not even a crack in it. She entered the room next day at one o'clock, and the same crash took place, being heard by all in the house: she went in at 10 A.M. on another day, and the same thing happened, after which she refused to enter that room again.

Another night, after 11 P.M., the servant was washing up in the kitchen, when heavy footsteps were heard by the father and mother going upstairs, and across a lobby to the servant's room; the father searched the house, but could find no one. After that footsteps used to be heard regularly at that hour, though no one could ever be seen walking about.

The two elder sisters slept together, and used to see flames shooting up all over the floor, though there was no smell or heat; this used to be seen two or three nights at a time, chiefly in the one room. The first time the girls saw this one of them got up and went to her father in alarm, naturally thinking the room underneath must be on fire.

The two boys were moved to the haunted room [which one?], where they slept in one large bed with its head near the chimney-piece. The elder boy, aged about thirteen, put his watch on the mantelpiece, awoke about 2 A.M., and wishing to ascertain the time, put his hand up for his watch; he then felt a deathly cold hand laid on his. For the rest of that night the two boys were terrified by noises, apparently caused by two people rushing about the room fighting and knocking against the bed. About 6 A.M. they went to their father, almost in hysterics from terror, and refused to sleep there again. The eldest sister, not being nervous, was then given that room; she was, however, so disturbed by these noises that she begged her father to let her leave it, but having no other room to give her, he persuaded her to stay there, and at length she got accustomed to the noise, and could sleep in spite of it. Finally the family left the house before their time was up.[7]

---

[7] *Journal of American S.P.R.* for September 1913.

A lady sends an account of curious experiences in a Co. Tipperary mansion, which seem to be a blending of ordinary haunting and death-warnings.

"Twelve years ago last spring the lady who then owned this place died, and about a week before her death a lady, who was staying in the house at the time, declared that she saw the figure of a woman in white fade into the opposite wall as she opened the door of a bedroom. We did not believe her story, and put it down to imagination.

"No death occurred in the house until last January, when an old man, who had lived here for some time, died. He had been ill here since the end of November, and died here on the 8th of January. Some time between Christmas Day and that date I went into the room where the white lady had been seen twelve years previously. It was about eleven o'clock at night, and I had no light with me. I walked towards a bed which stood in the centre of the room, when suddenly I became aware of a figure at the opposite side of it. I stood still, and stared at it. Neither of us uttered a word, but I knew from her appearance that she was not of this world.

"She was an old woman, yet not bent with years, but holding herself erect. Round her shoulders, which were plump and square, she had what appeared to be a black lace shawl. She had a thin veil over her face, so none of her features were clearly defined except her chin, which was remarkably long and pointed. Her head was covered with white curls, and a ribbon, also white, was passed round her forehead, and tied at the left side very stylishly in a bow. But the most peculiar point to be noticed was this—her head was outlined, not along the ribbon, but across the curls, by a row of faintly glimmering stars, which became smaller as they hung down at the bow. These were not arranged like a crown or tiara, but seemed as if the purpose was to light up the head. As you may perceive, I stood for some little time and took in every detail of her appearance. The room was in darkness, save for a faint light that came in from a passage through the open door behind me. But the ghostly figure was sufficiently lit up, not merely by the row of glimmering stars, but by a faint aura of light as well, which outlined all the body. When I had gazed at her for a sufficient time I thought I would go and get a candle, in the hope of seeing more clearly. I hurried away in search of one, but, of course, on my return the figure had vanished.

"Since beholding that vision some friends took me to a house some twenty-five miles away. There I happened to see an old portrait of a girl with powdered hair hanging down in curly ringlets, and a very long chain, though it represented a person many years younger than the figure I had seen. I do not know the lady of the house very well, but I managed to find out that the original of the portrait was a girl named Fitzgerald. I know that my great-grandmother had a friend of that name, a Mrs. Fitzgerald, who lived at Mitchelstown, and was styled 'The Wise Woman.' I am sure there is some connection between the portrait and the ghost, but unfortunately I am unable to trace it."

Mrs. Houlihan, now of the National Bank House, Thurles, has related to the present writer her experiences in a haunted house in Co. Kilkenny.

"When we were first married my husband was stationed in a town in Co. Kilkenny. He was with an accountant in the Bank, and as no official residence was allotted to us we had to rent a private house, which we got through a local house-agent. When letting it to us the agent said nothing about rumoured hauntings, while such a thing never entered my head. In our bedroom there was a large bed, with its head against the wall, and close beside it was a door leading into a dressing-room. One night my husband was away; I went to bed and fell sound asleep, but woke up suddenly to find the figure of a woman bending over me as I lay in bed. She was dressed in black, with an old-fashioned black bonnet, but her face seemed blurred and I was unable to distinguish her features. I stared at her in that half-unconscious way that one does when between sleeping and waking, and as I did so, the figure receded towards the middle of the room and then melted away. I told this experience to my husband, but he only laughed at it, and said it was due to imagination. However, some little time afterwards, I was away, and my husband was all alone. When I returned, he said to me, 'That story of yours was not all imagination, as I supposed. I have had exactly the same experience myself!'

"My husband frequently sat up late at night reading after I had gone to bed. He told me that many times he had the greatest difficulty to keep himself from looking over his shoulder to see who was coming into the room. He never saw or heard anything, but had this indefinable impulse to look round. One night I was in bed, with the lighted candle beside me, when suddenly there came a puff! And the candle was extinguished. It was not a gust of wind that quenched it, for I distinctly heard the sound as if a human being had blown it out.

"When I was alone in that room I always had an eerie uncomfortable feeling as if something supernatural was present. I found, however, by chance, that if I altered to the position of the bed I never experienced this sensation. So if I was left alone I would place the head of the bed towards another wall, and then I found that I slept without any feelings of uneasiness. But this eerie sensation was not confined to this one room; we used to put visitors into what was known as the spare room, and always, after the first night or so, they used to ask if they might have the dog to sleep with them, as there seemed to be something weird and uncanny about the room. When we were leaving the house the agent asked the maid if we hadn't seen the ghost! I had told her nothing of our experiences, so she was able to say truthfully that we had not."

The late Mr. T. J. Westropp, to whom we were indebted for so much material, sent a tale which used to be related by a relative of his, the Rev. Thomas Westropp, concerning experiences in a house not very far from the city of Limerick. When the latter was appointed to a certain parish he had some difficulty in finding a suitable house, but finally fixed on one which had been untenanted for many years, but had nevertheless been kept aired and in good repair, as a caretaker who lived close by used to come and look after it every day. The first night that the family settled there, as the clergyman was going upstairs he heard a footstep and the rustle of a dress, and as he stood aside a lady passed him, entered a door facing the stairs, and closed it after her. It was only then he realised that her dress was very old-fashioned, and that he had not been able to enter that particular room. Next day he got assistance from a carpenter, who, with another man, forced open the door. A mat of cobwebs fell as they did so, and the floor and windows were thick with dust. The men went across the room, and as the clergyman followed them he saw a small white bird flying round the ceiling; at his exclamation the men looked back and also saw it. It swooped, flew out of the door, and they did not see it again. After that the family were alarmed by hearing noises under the floor of that room every night. At length the clergyman had the boards taken up, and the skeleton of a child was found underneath. So old did the remains appear that the coroner did not deem it necessary to hold an inquest on them, so the rector buried them in the churchyard. Strange noises continued, as if someone were trying to force up the boards from underneath. Also a heavy ball was heard rolling down the stairs and striking against the study door. One night the two girls woke up screaming, and on the nurse running up to them, the elder said she had seen a great black dog with fiery eyes resting its paws on her bed. Her father ordered the servants to sit constantly with them in the evenings, but, notwithstanding the presence of two women in the nursery, the same thing occurred. The younger daughter was so scared that she never quite recovered. The family left the house immediately.

The same correspondent says: "An old ruined house in the hills of east Co. Clare enjoyed the reputation of being 'desperately haunted' from, at any rate, 1865 down to its dismantling. I will merely give the experiences of my own relations, as told by them to me. My mother told how one night she and my father heard creaking and grating, as if a door were being forced open. The sound came from a passage in which was a door nailed up and clamped with iron bands. A heavy footstep came down the passage, and stopped at the bedroom door for a moment; no sound was heard, and then the 'thing' came through the room to the foot of the bed. It moved round the bed, they not daring to stir. The horrible unseen visitant stopped, and they *felt* it watching them. At last it moved away, they heard it going up the passage, the door crashed, and all was silence. Lighting a candle, my father examined the room, and found the door locked; he then went along the passage, but not a sound was to be heard anywhere.

"Strange noises like footsteps, sobbing, whispering, grim laughter, and shrieks were often heard about the house. On one occasion my eldest sister and a girl cousin drove over to see the family and stayed the night. They and my two younger sisters were all crowded into a huge, old-fashioned bed, and carefully drew and tucked in the curtains all round. My eldest sister awoke feeling a cold wind blowing on her face, and putting out her hand found the curtains drawn back and, as they subsequently discovered, wedged between the bed and the wall. She reached for the match-box, and was about to light the candle when a horrible mocking laugh rang out close to the bed, which awakened the other girls. Being always a plucky woman, though then badly scared, she struck a match, and searched the room, but nothing was to be seen. The closed room was said to have been deserted after a murder, and its floor was supposed to be stained with blood which no human power could wash out."

Another house in Co. Clare, nearer the estuary of the Shannon, which was formerly the residence of the D— family, but is now pulled down, had some extraordinary tales told about it in which facts (if we may use the word) were well supplemented by legend. To commence with the former. A lady writes: "My father and old Mr. D— were first cousins. Richard D— asked my father would he come and sit up with him one night, in order to see what might be seen. Both were particularly sober men. The annoyances in the house were becoming unbearable. Mrs. D—'s work-box used to be thrown down, the table-cloth would be whisked off the table, the fender and fire-irons would be hurled about the room, and other similar things would happen. Mr. D— and my father went up to one of the bedrooms, where a big fire was made up. They searched every part of the room carefully, but nothing uncanny was to be seen or found. They then placed two candles and a brace of pistols on a small table between them, and waited. Nothing happened for some time, till all of a sudden a large black dog walked out from under the bed. Both men fired, and the dog disappeared. That is all! The family had to leave the house."

Now to the blending of fact with fiction, of which we have already spoken: the intelligent reader can decide in his own mind which is which. It was said that black magic had been practised in this house at one time, and that in consequence terrible and weird occurrences were quite the order of the day there. When being cooked, the hens used to scream and the mutton used to bleat in the pot. Black dogs were seen frequently. The beds used to be lifted up, and the occupants thereof used to be beaten black and blue, by invisible hands. One particularly ghoulish tale was told. It was said that a monk (!) was in love with one of the daughters of the house, who was an exceedingly fat girl. She died unmarried, and was buried in the family vault. Some time later the vault was again opened for an interment, and those who entered it found that Miss D—'s coffin had been disturbed, and the lid loosened. They then saw that all the fat around her heart had been scooped away.

Apropos of ineradicable blood on a floor, which is a not infrequent item in stories of haunted houses, it is said that a manifestation of this nature forms the haunting in a farmhouse in Co. Limerick. According to our informants, a light must be kept burning in this house all night; if by any chance it is forgotten, or becomes quenched, in the morning the floor is covered with blood. The story is evidently much older than the house, but no traditional explanation is given.

Two stories of haunted schools have been sent to us, both on very good authority; these establishments lie within the geographical limits of this chapter, but for obvious reasons, we cannot indicate their locality more precisely, though the names of both are known to us. The first of these was told to our correspondent by the boy Brown, who was in the room, but did not see the ghost.

When Brown was about fifteen he was sent to —— School. His brother told him not to be frightened at anything he might see or hear, as the boys were sure to play tricks on all newcomers. He was put to sleep in a room with another new arrival, a boy named Smith, from England. In the middle of the night Brown was roused from his sleep by Smith crying out in great alarm, and asking who was in the room. Brown, who was very angry at being waked up, told him not to be a fool—that there was no one there. The second night Smith roused him again, this time in greater alarm than the first night. He said he saw a man in cap and gown come into the room with a lamp, and then pass right through the wall. Smith got out of his bed, and fell on his knees beside Brown, beseeching him not to go to sleep. At first Brown thought it was all done to frighten him, but he then saw that Smith was in a state of abject terror. Next morning they spoke of the occurrence, and the report reached the ears of the Head Master, who sent for the two boys. Smith refused to spend another night in the room. Brown said he had seen or heard nothing, and was quite willing to sleep there if another fellow would sleep with him, but he would not care to remain there alone. The Head Master then asked for volunteers from the class of elder boys, but not one of them would sleep in the room. It had always been looked upon as "haunted," but the Master thought that by putting in new boys who had not heard the story they would sleep there all right.

Some years after, Brown revisited the place, and found that another attempt had been made to occupy the room. A new Head Master who did not know its history, thought it a pity to have the room idle, and put a teacher, also new to the school, in possession. When this teacher came down the first morning, he asked who had come into his room during the night. He stated that a man in cap and gown, having books under his arm and a lamp in his hand, came in, sat down at a table, and began to read. He knew that he was not one of the masters, and did not recognise him as one of the boys. The room had to be abandoned. The tradition is that many years ago a master was murdered in that room by one of the students. The few boys who ever had the courage to persist in sleeping in the room said if they stayed more than two or three nights that the furniture was moved, and they heard violent noises.

The second story was sent to us by the percipient herself, and is therefore a first-hand experience. Considering that she was only a schoolgirl at the time, it must be admitted that she made a most plucky attempt to run the ghost to earth.

"A good many years ago, when I first went to school, I did not believe in ghosts, but I then had an experience which caused me to alter my opinion. I was ordered with two other girls to sleep in a small top room at the back of the house which overlooked a garden which contained ancient apple trees.

"Suddenly in the dead of night I was awakened out of my sleep by the sound of heavy footsteps, as of a man wearing big boots unlaced, pacing ceaselessly up and down a long corridor which I knew was plainly visible from the landing outside my door, as there was a large window at the farther end of it, and there was sufficient moonlight to enable one to see its full length. After listening for about twenty minutes, my curiosity was aroused, so I got up and stood on the landing. The footsteps still continued, but I could see nothing, although the sounds actually reached the foot of the flight of stairs which led from the corridor to the landing on which I was standing. Suddenly the footfall ceased, pausing at my end of the corridor, and I then considered it was high time for me to retire, which I accordingly did, carefully closing the door behind me.

"To my horror the footsteps ascended the stairs, and the bedroom door was violently dashed back against a washing-stand, beside which was a bed; the contents of the ewer were spilled over the occupant, and the steps advanced a few paces into the room in my direction. A cold perspiration broke out all over me; I cannot describe the sensation. It was not actual fear—it was more than that—I felt I had come into contact with the Unknown.

"What was about to happen? All I could do was to speak; I cried out, "Who are you? What do you want?" Suddenly the footsteps ceased; I felt relieved, and lay awake till morning, but no further sound reached my ears. How or when my ghostly visitant disappeared I never knew; suffice it to say, my story was no nightmare, but an actual fact, of which there was found sufficient proof in the morning: the floor was still saturated with water; the door, which we always carefully closed at night, was wide open; and last, but not least, the occupant of the wet bed had heard all that had happened, but feared to speak, and lay awake till morning.

"Naturally, we related our weird experience to our schoolmates, and it was only then I learned from one of the elder girls that this ghost had manifested itself for many years in a similar fashion to the inhabitants of that room. It was supposed to be the spirit of a man who, long years before, had occupied this apartment (the house was then a private residence), and had committed suicide by hanging himself from an old apple tree opposite the window. Needless to say, the story was hushed up, and we were sharply spoken to, and warned not to mention the occurrence again.

"Some years afterwards a friend, who happened at the time to be a boarder at this very school, came to spend a week-end with me. She related an exactly similar incident which occurred a few nights previous to her visit. My experience was quite unknown to her."

The following account of strange happenings at his glebe-house has been sent by the rector of a parish in the diocese of Cashel: "Shortly after my wife and I came to live here, some ten years ago, the servants complained of hearing strange noises in the top storey of the Rectory where they sleep. One girl ran away the day after she arrived, declaring that the house was haunted, and that nothing would induce her to sleep another night in it. So often had my wife to change servants on this account that at last I had to speak to the parish priest, as I suspected that the idea of 'ghosts' might have been suggested to the maids by neighbours who might have some interest in getting rid of them. I understand that my friend the parish priest spoke very forcibly from the altar on the subject of spirits, saying that the only spirits he believed ever did any harm to anyone were ——— , mentioning a well-known brand of the wine of the country. Whether this priestly admonition was the cause or not, for some time we heard no more tales of ghostly manifestations.

"After a while, however, my wife and I began to hear a noise which, while in no sense alarming, has proved to be both remarkable and inexplicable. If we happen to be sitting in the dining-room after dinner, sometimes we hear what sounds like the noise of a heavy coach rumbling up to the hall door. We have both heard this noise hundreds of times between eight P.M. and midnight. Sometimes we hear it several times the same night, and then perhaps we won't hear it again for several months. We hear it best on calm nights, and as we are nearly a quarter of a mile from the high road, it is difficult to account for, especially as the noise appears to be quite close to us—I mean not farther away than the hall-door. I may mention that an Englishman was staying with us a few years ago. As we were sitting in the dining-room one night after dinner he said, 'A carriage has just driven up to the door'; but we knew it was only the 'phantom coach,' for we also heard it. Only once do I remember hearing it while sitting in the drawing-room. So much for the 'sound' of the 'phantom coach' but now I must tell you what I *saw* with my own eyes as clearly as I now see the paper on which I am writing. Some years ago in the middle of the summer, on a scorching hot day, I was out cutting some hay opposite the hall door just by the tennis court. It was between twelve and one o'clock. I remember the time distinctly, as my man had gone to his dinner shortly before. The spot on which I was commanded a view of the avenue from the entrance gate for about four hundred yards. I happened to look up from my occupation—for scything is no easy work—and I saw what I took to be a somewhat high dogcart, in which two people were seated, turning in at the avenue gate. As I had my coat and waistcoat off, and was not in a state to receive visitors, I got behind a newly-made hay-cock and watched the vehicle until it came to a bend in the avenue where there is a clump of trees which obscured it from my view. As it did not, however, reappear, I concluded that the occupants had either stopped for some reason or had taken by mistake a cart-way leading to the back gate into the garden. Hastily putting on my coat, I went down to the bend in the avenue, but to my surprise there was nothing to be seen.

"Returning to the Rectory, I met my housekeeper, who has been with me for nearly twenty years, and I told her what I had seen. She then told me that about a month before, while I was away from home, my man had one day gone with the trap to the station. She saw, just as I did, a trap coming up the avenue until it was lost to sight owing to the intervention of the clump of trees. As it did not come on, she went down to the bend, but there was no trap to be seen. When the man came in some half-hour after, my housekeeper asked him if he had come half-way up the avenue and turned back, but he said he had only that minute come straight from the station. My housekeeper said she did not like to tell me about it before, as she thought I 'would have laughed at her.' Whether the 'spectral gig' which I saw and the 'phantom coach' which my wife and I have often heard are one and the same I know not, but I do know that what I saw in the full blaze of the summer sun was not inspired by a dose of the spirits referred to by my friend the parish priest.

" Some time during the winter of 1912, I was in the motor-house one dark evening at about 6 P.M. I was working at the engine, and as the car was 'nose in' first, I was, of course, at the farthest point from the door. I had sent my man down to the village with a message. He was gone about ten minutes when I heard heavy footsteps enter the yard and come over to the motor-house. I 'felt' that there was someone in the house quite close to me, and I said, 'Hullo, ——, what brought you back so soon,' as I knew he could not have been to the village and back. As I got no reply, I took up my electric lamp and went to the back of the motor to see who was there, but there was no one to be seen, and although I searched the yard with my lamp, I could discover no one. About a week later I heard the footsteps again under almost identical conditions, but I searched with the same futile result.

"Before I stop, I must tell you about a curious 'presentiment' which happened with regard to a man I got from the Queen's County. He arrived on a Saturday evening, and on the following

Monday morning I put him to sweep the avenue. He was at his work when I went out in the motor car at about 10.30 A.M. Shortly after I left he left his wheel-barrow and tools on the avenue (just at the point where I saw the 'spectral gig' disappear) and, coming up to the Rectory, he told my housekeeper in a great state of agitation that he was quite sure that his brother, with whom he had always lived, was dead. He said he must return home at once. My housekeeper advised him to wait until I returned, but he changed his clothes and packed his box, saying he must catch the next train. Just before I returned home at 12 o'clock, a telegram came saying his brother had died suddenly that morning, and that he was to return at once. On my return I found him almost in a state of collapse. He left by the next train, and I never heard of him again."

K— Castle is a handsome blending of ancient castle and modern dwelling-house, picturesquely situated among trees, while the steep glen mentioned below runs close beside it. It has the reputation of being haunted, but, as usual, it is difficult to get information. One gentleman, to whom we wrote, stated that he never saw or heard anything worse than a bat. On the other hand, a lady who resided there a good many years ago, gives the following account of her extraordinary experiences therein:

DEAR MR. SEYMOUR,

I enclose some account of our experiences in K— Castle. It would be better not to mention names, as the people occupying it have told me they are afraid of their servants hearing anything, and consequently giving notice. They themselves hear voices often, but, like me, they do not mind. When first we went there we heard people talking, but on looking everywhere we could find no one. Then on some nights we heard fighting in the glen beside the house. We could hear voices raised in anger, and the clash of steel: no person would venture there after dusk.

One night I was sitting talking with my governess, I got up, said good-night, and opened the door, which was on the top of the back staircase. As I did so, I *heard* someone (a woman) come slowly upstairs, walk past us to a window at the end of the landing, and then with a shriek fall heavily. As she passed it was bitterly cold, and I drew back into the room, but did not say anything, as it might frighten the governess. She asked me what was the matter, as I looked so white. Without answering, I pushed her into her room, and then searched the house, but with no results.

Another night I was sleeping with my little girl. I awoke, and saw a girl with long, fair hair standing at the fireplace, one hand at her side, the other on the chimney-piece. Thinking at first it was my little girl, I felt on the pillow to see if she were gone, but she was fast asleep. There was no fire or light of any kind in the room.

Some time afterwards a friend was sleeping there, and she told me that she was pushed out of bed the whole night. Two gentlemen to whom I had mentioned this came over, thinking they would find out the cause. In the morning when they came down they asked for the carriage to take them to the next train, but would not tell what they had heard or seen. Another person who came to visit her sister, who was looking after the house before we went in, slept in this room, and in the morning said she must go back that day. She also would give no information.

On walking down the corridor, I have heard a door open, a footstep cross before me, and go into another room, *both* doors being closed at the time. An old cook I had told me that when she went into the hall in the morning, a gentleman would come down the front stairs, take a plumed hat off the stand, and vanish *through* the hall door. This she saw nearly every morning. She also said that a girl often came into her bedroom, and put her hand on her (the cook's) face; and when she would push her away she would hear a girl's voice say, "Oh don't!" three times. I have often heard voices in the drawing-room, which decidedly sounded as if an old gentleman and a girl were talking. Noises like furniture being moved were frequently heard at night, and strangers staying with us have often asked why the servants turned out the rooms underneath them at such an unusual hour. The front-door bell sometimes rang, and I have gone down, but found no one.—Yours very sincerely,

F. T.

In one of the most southern counties of Ireland—for unfortunately we are precluded from giving any closer indication of place—there stands a castle, not hoary with age, but a modern antique, though as stoutly and strongly built as if it dated from the days of yore, which is said to have been erected by an eccentric member of a titled family. This castle is surrounded by a spacious walled-in courtyard, to which admission is obtained through a large gateway. The entrance-door of this castle is approached by two or three steps. On entering, the visitor finds that a flight of steps on his left leads down to a basement or cellar. A short straight flight of stone steps on his right conducts him to the hall; while the upper storeys are reached by a stone staircase, not spiral, as is usually the case, but straight, though the flights go in a somewhat zigzag manner.

The place is haunted by a peculiar noise, which is heard periodically. A gentleman, whom the present writer has known intimately from childhood, relates his experience of this noise as follows:

"My regiment went out for training every summer to this castle, and our tents were pitched inside the courtyard. One night two or three other officers and myself were standing in the courtyard chatting before retiring to our respective tents. We were only a few yards from the entrance-door of the castle, and our thoughts were on anything save ghosts. The night was perfectly still. Suddenly we heard within the castle a most appalling uproar. It sounded exactly as if someone had filled a clothes-basket with crockery and then flung the contents headlong down the stone stairs. Crash! Crash! Crash! The imaginary china seemed to be rattling and leaping from step to step until it reached the hall, or thereabouts, when it ceased as suddenly as it had begun. On the moment we determined to investigate the matter. We rushed to the entrance-door, but finding this locked, managed to make our way in through a window. We then closely examined the entire building from top to bottom, but found nothing out of place or damaged. Some of the rooms were used as offices by us, and the furniture was not stirred. There was even some china belonging to the regiment stored there, and this we found absolutely intact. So we made our way out again, no nearer the solution of the mystery than when we entered.

"I have heard the noise myself, and so have others, on different occasions during our periods of training. It always seems as if it commenced at the very top of the building, which was four storeys high (not counting the basement), as well as I remember, and continued until it reached the hall or thereabouts; it never appeared to go down into the cellar. Sometimes the noise lasted as long as it would take an imaginary basket full of china to fall the distance I have mentioned; at other times it seemed to last somewhat longer. It was always heard at night, never in the daytime, so far as I am aware. We got quite used to it in time, and when we heard it used to say, 'Oh, there's the ghost at it again!'"

"Kilman" Castle, in the heart of Ireland—the name is obviously a pseudonym—has been described as perhaps the worst haunted mansion in the British Isles. That it deserves this doubtful recommendation, we cannot say; but at all events the ordinary reader will be prepared to admit that it contains sufficient "ghosts" to satisfy the most greedy ghost-hunter. A couple of months ago the present writer paid a visit to this castle, and was shown all over it one morning by the mistress of the house, who, under the *nom de plume* of "Andrew Merry" has published novels dealing with Irish life, and has also contributed articles on the ghostly phenomena of her house to the *Occult Review* (Dec. 1908 and Jan. 1909).

The place itself is a grim, grey, bare building. The central portion, in which is the entrance-hall, is a square castle of the usual type; it is built on a rock, and a slight batter from base to summit gives an added appearance of strength and solidity. On either side of the castle are more modern wings, one of which terminates in what is known as the "Priest's House."

Now to the ghosts. The top storey of the central tower is a large, well-lighted apartment, called the "Chapel," having evidently served that purpose in times past. At one end is what is said to be an *oubliette*, now almost filled up. Occasionally in the evenings, people walking along the roads or in the fields see the windows of this chapel lighted up for a few seconds as if many lamps were suddenly brought into it. This is certainly *not* due to servants; from our experience we can testify that it is the last place on earth that a domestic would enter after dark. It is also said that a treasure is buried somewhere in or around the castle. The legend runs that an ancestor was about to be taken to Dublin on a charge of rebellion, and, fearing he would never return, made the best of the time left to him by burying somewhere a crock full of gold and jewels. Contrary to expectation, he *did* return; but his long confinement had turned his brain, and he could never remember the spot where he had deposited his treasure years before. Some time ago a lady, a Miss B., who was decidedly psychic, was invited to Kilman Castle in the hope that she would be able to locate the whereabouts of this treasure. In this respect she failed, unfortunately, but gave, nevertheless, a curious example of her power. As she walked through the hall with her hostess, she suddenly laid her hand upon the bare stone wall, and remarked, "There is something uncanny here, but I don't know what it is." In that very spot, some time previously, two skeletons had been discovered walled up.

The sequel to this is curious. Some time after, Miss B. was either trying automatic writing, or else was at a séance (we forget which), when a message came to her from the Unseen, stating that the treasure at Kilman Castle was concealed in the chapel under the tessellated pavement near the altar. But this spirit was either a "lying spirit," or else a most impish one, for there is no trace of an altar, and it is impossible to say, from the style of the room, where it stood; while the tessellated pavement (if it exists) is so covered with the debris of the former roof that it would be almost impossible to have it thoroughly cleared.

There is as well a miscellaneous assortment of ghosts. A monk with tonsure and cowl walks in at one window of the Priest's House, and out at another. There is also a little old man, dressed in the antique garb of a green cut-away coat, knee breeches, and buckled shoes: he is sometimes accompanied by an old lady in similar old-fashioned costume. Another ghost has a penchant for lying on the bed beside its lawful and earthly occupant; nothing is seen, but a great weight is felt, and a consequent deep impression made on the bedclothes.

The lady of the house states that she has a number of letters from friends, in which they relate the supernatural experiences they had while staying at the Castle. In one of these the writer, a gentleman, was awakened one night by an extraordinary feeling of intense cold at his heart. He then saw in front of him a tall female figure, clothed from head to foot in red, and with its right hand raised menacingly in the air: the light which illuminated the figure was from within. He lit a match, and sprang out of bed, but the room was empty. He went back to bed, and saw nothing more that night, except that several times the same cold feeling gripped his heart, though to the touch the flesh was quite warm.

But of all the ghosts in that well-haunted house the most unpleasant is that inexplicable thing that is usually called "It." The lady of the house described to the present writer her personal experience of this phantom. High up round one side of the hall runs a gallery which connects with some of the bedrooms. One evening she was in this gallery leaning on the balustrade, and looking down into the hall. Suddenly she felt two hands laid on her shoulders; she turned round sharply, and saw "It" standing close beside her. She described it as being human in shape, and about four feet high; the eyes were like two black holes in the face, and the whole figure seemed as if it were made of grey cotton-wool, while it was accompanied by a most appalling stench, such as would come from a decaying human body. The lady got a shock from which she did not recover for a long time.

An even more unpleasant account of a haunting[8] was told to Mr. Reginald B. Span by the Rev. F. Bennet, of the Anglican Church, Arizona, U.S.A. Some friends of the latter's rented an old castle in the South of Ireland—a very ancient and picturesque building standing in beautiful and extensive grounds. They heard some rumours of the place being haunted, but as they were getting it at a low rent this did not concern them.

The new tenants, the A. family, were delighted with their new residence, and for some time nothing uncanny was noticed. After a little, however, the servants complained of footsteps outside their doors and of someone attempting to enter their rooms, but this was put down to imagination induced by the tales told to them by the village people. One night Mrs A. was late in retiring— her husband had gone to Dublin—and was sitting by her bedroom fire. Perfect stillness reigned through the house. Suddenly the silence was broken by the sharp bang of a door in the corridor where the room was, followed by the sound of footsteps—but most peculiar footsteps—moving in a stealthy way down the corridor. She opened the door, and went outside with a lighted candle to see who or what it was. At the end of the passage she saw in the dim light an extraordinary-looking figure moving with a clumsy, shambling, but stealthy tread towards the staircase. She

---

[8]   *Occult Review*, vol. iv. p.197.

held the light above her head to get a better view, and the creature turned around for an instant and looked at her, disclosing a human face of revolting hideousness surmounting what appeared to be the body of a huge ape—and then in an instant it vanished.

Shrieking with terror she rushed back to her room. One of her daughters came hurriedly in at the outcry, and on learning what had been seen, tried to persuade her mother that it was nothing but a nightmare. The next day Mr A. returned, and his wife decided to say nothing to him about her experience.

A few nights later Mr. A. was coming up the stairs from the big entrance-hall, where he had been smoking and reading before retiring, when he heard a weird, blood-curdling sort of love, and looking up to the landing above saw a tall ungainly figure leaning over the banisters looking down at him. He saw its face distinctly, which was that of a man of about forty years of age—deathly white and hairless—with the most horribly malignant expression. At that moment the features were distorted by a hideous grin, and the form shook with laughter, while the eyes seemed to gleam like red-hot coals. The hands and arms resting on the rail of the banister were like those of an ape, while the whole form was covered with thick reddish-brown hair. Mr. A. rushed up the stairs towards it, whereupon it gave peal after peal of the fiendish laughter, and then vanished.

Mrs. A. and her son and daughter heard the noise of laughing, and they joined Mr. A., who recounted his experience, whereupon Mrs. A. told what had befallen her a few nights previously. They thereupon determined to search all the rooms, which they did thoroughly without finding a trace of anything. As the servants occupied another part of the house they had heard nothing, and of course were kept in ignorance. They decided that they would not relinquish the tenancy, but determined to keep a sharp look-out and try and get at the bottom of the mystery. Nothing further happened for some time. There were occasionally queer noises heard in the early hours of morning, such as footsteps, muffled cries and groans, and banging of doors, none of which they could account for, but which did not disturb them much.

However, a climax came which caused them to leave. Miss A. was one afternoon in the drawing-room arranging some flowers. She was standing at one of the tables when she heard a noise behind her, and felt two hands laid on her shoulders. Thinking it was a girl friend who was then in the house she exclaimed lightly, "Oh, there you are!" and on turning round to greet her, came face to face with a most loathsome-looking creature which had just removed its hands from her shoulders and was chuckling with diabolical glee. It was neither human being nor animal—and instead of clothing was covered with hair like an orang-outang: it stood over six feet high and had a most repulsive appearance. It was, in fact, the creature which had been seen twice before, at night-time. Feeling sick and faint with horror and disgust she gave a piercing shriek, and just as her friend entered the room the apparition disappeared, and Miss A. fell back in a dead faint. The girl who came in so opportunely just caught a glimpse of the ghost before it vanished. After this episode the A.s thought it would be advisable to go, and accordingly left T— Castle as soon as they conveniently could.

IV

POLTERGEISTS

POLTERGEIST is the term assigned to those apparently meaningless noises and movements of objects of which we from time to time hear accounts. The word is, of course, German, and may be translated "boisterous ghost." A poltergeist is seldom or never seen, but contents itself by moving furniture and other objects about in an extraordinary manner, often contrary to the laws of gravitation; sometimes footsteps are heard, but nothing is visible, while at other times vigorous rappings will be heard either on the walls or floor of a room, and in the manner in which the raps are given a poltergeist has often showed itself as having a close connection with the physical phenomena of spiritualism, for cases have occurred in which a poltergeist has given the exact number of raps mentally asked for by some person present. Another point that is worthy of note is the fact that the hauntings of a poltergeist are generally attached to a certain individual in a certain spot, and thus differ from the operations of an ordinary ghost.

The two following incidents related in this chapter are taken from a paper read by Professor Barrett, F.R.S., before the Society for Psychical Research.[9] In the case of the first anecdote he made

---

[9]   Proceedings, August 1911, pp. 377–95.

every possible inquiry into the facts set forth, short of actually being an eye-witness of the phenomena. In the case of the second he made personal investigation, and himself saw the whole of the incidents related. There is therefore very little room to doubt the genuineness of either story.

In the year 1910, in a certain house in Court Street, Enniscorthy, there lived a labouring man named Redmond. His wife took in boarders to supplement her husband's wages, and at the time to which we refer there were three men boarding with her, who slept in one room above the kitchen. The house consisted of five rooms—two on the ground-floor, of which one was a shop and the other the kitchen. The two other rooms upstairs were occupied by the Redmonds and their servant respectively. The bedroom in which the boarders slept was large, and contained two beds, one at each end of the room, two men sleeping in one of them; John Randall and George Sinnott were the names of two, but the name of the third lodger is not known—he seems to have left the Redmonds very shortly after the disturbances commenced.

It was on July 4, 1910, that John Randall, who is a carpenter by trade, went to live at Enniscorthy, and took rooms with the Redmonds. In a signed statement, now in possession of Professor Barrett, he tells a graphic tale of what occurred each night during the three weeks he lodged in the house, and as a result of the poltergeist's attentions he lost three-quarters of a stone in weight. It was on the night of Thursday, July 7, that the first incident occurred, when the bedclothes were gently pulled off his bed. Of course he naturally thought it was a joke, and shouted to his companions to stop. As no one could explain what was happening, a match was struck, and the bedclothes were found to be at the window, from which the other bed (a large piece of furniture which ordinarily took two people to move) had been rolled just when the clothes had been taken off Randall's bed. Things were put straight and the light blown out, "but," Randall's account goes on to say, "it wasn't long until we heard some hammering in the room—tap-tap-tap-like. This lasted for a few minutes, getting quicker and quicker. When it got very quick, their bed started to move out across the room. . . . We then struck a match and got the lamp. We searched the room thoroughly, and could find nobody. Nobody had come in the door. We called the man of the house (Redmond); he came into the room, saw the bed, and told us to push it back and get into bed (he thought all the time one of us was playing the trick on the other). I said I wouldn't stay in the other bed by myself, so I got in with the others; we put out the light again, and it had only been a couple of minutes out when the bed ran out on the floor with the three of us. Richard struck a match again, and this time we all got up and put on our clothes; we had got a terrible fright and couldn't stick it any longer. We told the man of the house we would sit up in the room till daylight. During the time we were sitting in the room we could hear footsteps leaving the kitchen and coming up the stairs; it would stop on the landing outside the door, and wouldn't come into the room. The footsteps and noises continued through the house until daybreak."

The next night the footsteps and noises were continued, but the unfortunate men did not experience any other annoyance. On the following day the men went home, and it is to be hoped they were able to make up for all the sleep they had lost on the two previous nights. They returned on the Sunday, and from that night till they finally left the house the men were disturbed practically every night. On Monday, 11th July the bed was continually running out from the wall with its three occupants. They kept the lamp alight, and a chair was seen to dance gaily out into the middle of the floor. On the following Thursday we read of the same happenings, with the addition that one of the boarders was lifted out of the bed, though he felt no hand near him. It seems strange that they should have gone through such a bad night exactly a week from the night the poltergeist started its operations. So the account goes on; every night that they slept in the room the hauntings continued, some nights being worse than others. On Friday, 29th July, "the bed turned up on one side and threw us out on the floor, and before we were thrown out, the pillow was taken from under my head three times. When the bed rose up, it fell back without making any noise. This bed was so heavy, it took both the woman and the girl to pull it out from the wall without anybody in it, and there were only three castors on it." The poltergeist must have been an insistent fellow, for when the unfortunate men took refuge in the other bed, they had not been long in it before it began to rise, but could not get out of the recess it was in unless it was taken to pieces.

"It kept very bad," we read, "for the next few nights. So Mr. Murphy, from the *Guardian* office, and another man named Devereux, came and stopped in the room one night."

The experiences of Murphy and Devereux on this night are contained in a further statement, signed by Murphy and corroborated by Devereux. They seem to have gone to work in a business-like manner, as before taking their positions for the night they made a complete investigation of the bedroom and house, so as to eliminate all chance of trickery or fraud. By this time, it should be noted, one of Mrs. Redmond's lodgers had evidently suffered enough from the poltergeist, as only two men are mentioned in Murphy's statement, one sleeping in each bed. The two investigators took up their position against the wall midway between the two beds, so that they had a full view of the room and the occupants of the beds. "The night," says Murphy, "was a clear, starlight night. No blind obstructed the view from outside, and one could see the outlines of the beds and their occupants clearly. At about 11.30 a tapping was heard close at the foot of Randall's bed. My companion remarked that it appeared to be like the noise of a rat eating at timber. Sinnott replied, 'You'll soon see the rat it is.' The tapping went on slowly at first . . . then the speed gradually increased to about a hundred or a hundred and twenty per minute, the noise growing louder. This continued for about five minutes, when it stopped suddenly. Randall then spoke. He said: 'The clothes are slipping off my bed: look at them sliding off. Good God, they are going off me.' Mr. Devereux immediately struck a match, which he had ready in his hand. The bedclothes had partly left the boy's bed, having gone diagonally towards the foot, going out at the left corner, and not alone did they seem to be drawn off the bed, but they appeared to be actually going back under the bed, much in the same position one would expect bed-clothes to be if a strong breeze were blowing through the room at the time. But then everything was perfectly calm."

A search was then made for wires or strings, but nothing of the sort could be found. The bedclothes were put back and the light extinguished. For ten minutes silence reigned, only to be broken by more rapping which was followed by shouts from Randall. He was told to hold on to the clothes, which were sliding off again. But this was of little use, for he was heard to cry, "I'm going, I'm going, I'm gone," and when a light was struck he was seen to slide from the bed and all the bedclothes with him. Randall, who, with Sinnott, had shown considerable strength of mind by staying in the house under such trying circumstances, had evidently had enough of ghostly hauntings, for as he lay on the floor, trembling in every limb and bathed in perspiration, he exclaimed: "Oh, isn't this dreadful? I can't stand it; I can't stay here any longer." He was eventually persuaded to get back to bed. Later on more rapping occurred in a different part of the room, but it soon stopped, and the rest of the night passed away in peace.

Randall and Sinnott went to their homes the next day, and Mr. Murphy spent from eleven till long past midnight in their vacated room, but heard and saw nothing unusual. He states in conclusion that "Randall could not reach that part of the floor from which the rapping came on any occasion without attracting my attention and that of my comrade."

The next case related by Professor Barrett occurred in County Fermanagh, at a spot eleven miles from Enniskillen and about two miles from the hamlet of Derrygonelly, where there dwelt a farmer and his family of four girls and a boy, of whom the eldest was a girl of about twenty years of age named Maggie. His cottage consisted of three rooms, the kitchen, or dwelling-room, being in the centre, with a room on each side used as bedrooms. In one of these two rooms Maggie slept with her sisters, and it was here that the disturbances occurred, generally after they had all gone to bed, when rappings and scratchings were heard which often lasted all night. Rats were first blamed, but when things were moved by some unseen agent, and boots and candles thrown out of the house, it was seen that something more than the ordinary rat was at work. The old farmer, who was a Methodist, sought advice from his class leader, and by his directions laid an open Bible on the bed in the haunted room, placing a big stone on the book. But the stone was lifted off by an unseen hand, the Bible moved out of the room, and seventeen pages torn out of it. They could not keep a lamp or candle in the house, so they went to their neighbours for help, and, to quote the old farmer's words to Professor Barrett, "Jack Flanigan came and lent us a lamp, saying the devil himself would not steal it, as he had got the priest to sprinkle it with holy water." "But that," the old man said, "did us no good either, for the next day it took away that lamp also."

Professor Barrett, at the invitation of Mr. Thomas Plunkett of Enniskillen, went to investigate. He got a full account from the farmer of the freakish tricks which were continually being played in the house, and gives a graphic account of what he himself observed: "After the children, except the boy, had gone to bed, Maggie lay down on the bed without undressing, so that her hands and feet could be observed. The rest of us sat round the kitchen fire, when faint raps, rapidly increasing in loudness, were heard coming apparently from the walls, the ceiling, and various parts of the inner room, the door of which was open. On entering the bedroom with a light the noises at first ceased, but recommenced when I put the light on the window-sill in the kitchen. I had the boy and his father by my side, and asked Mr. Plunkett to look round the house outside. Standing in the doorway leading to the bedroom, the noises recommenced, the light was gradually brought nearer, and after much patience I was able to bring the light into the bedroom whilst the disturbances were still loudly going on. At last I was able to go up to the side of the bed, with the lighted candle in my hand, and closely observed each of the occupants lying on the bed. The younger children were apparently asleep, and Maggie was motionless; nevertheless, knocks were going on everywhere around; on the chairs, the bedstead, the walls and ceiling. The closest scrutiny failed to detect any movement on the part of those present that could account for the noises, which were accompanied by a scratching or tearing sound. Suddenly a large pebble fell in my presence on to the bed; no one had moved to dislodge it, even if it had been placed for the purpose. When I replaced the candle on the window-sill in the kitchen, the knocks became still louder, like those made by a heavy carpenter's hammer driving nails into flooring."

A couple of days afterwards, the Rev. Maxwell Close, M.A., a well-known member of the S.P.R., joined Professor Barrett and Mr. Plunkett, and together the party of three paid visits on two consecutive nights to the haunted farmhouse, and the noises were repeated. Complete search was made, both inside and outside of the house, but no cause could be found. When the party were leaving, the old farmer was much perturbed that they had not "laid the ghost." When questioned he said he thought it was fairies. He was asked if it had answered to questions by raps and he said he had; "but it tells lies as often as truth, and oftener, I think. We tried it, and it only knocked at L M N when we said the alphabet over." Professor Barrett then tested it by asking mentally for a certain number of raps, and immediately the actual number was heard. He repeated this four times with a different number each time, and with the same result.

Perhaps the most interesting part of this particular case is at the end of Professor Barrett's account, when, at the request of the old farmer, Mr. Maxwell Close read some passages from Scripture, followed by the Lord's Prayer, to an accompaniment of knockings and scratches, which were at first so loud that the solemn words could hardly be heard, but which gradually ceased as they all knelt in prayer. And since that night no further disturbance occurred.

Another similar story comes from the north of Ireland. In the year 1866 (as recorded in the *Larne Reporter* of March 31 in that year), two families residing at Upper Ballygowan, near Larne, suffered a series of annoyances from having stones thrown into their houses both by night and by day. Their neighbours came in great numbers to sympathise with them in their affliction, and on one occasion, after a volley of stones had been poured into the house through the window, a young man who was present fired a musket in the direction of the mysterious assailants. The reply was a loud peal of satanic laughter, followed by a volley of stones and turf. On another occasion a heap of potatoes, which was in an inner apartment of one of the houses, was seen to be in commotion, and shortly afterwards its contents were hurled into the kitchen, where the inmates of the house, with some of their neighbours, were assembled.

The explanation given by some people of this mysterious affair was as mysterious as the affair itself. It was said that many years before the occurrences which we have now related took place, the farmer who then occupied the premises in which they happened was greatly annoyed by mischievous tricks which were played upon him by a company of fairies who had a habit of holding their rendezvous in his house. The consequence was that this man had to leave the house, which for a long time stood a roofless ruin. After the lapse of many years, and when the story about the dilapidated fabric having been haunted had probably been forgotten, the people who then occupied the adjoining lands unfortunately took some of the stones of the old deserted mansion to repair their own buildings. At this the fairies, or "good people," were much incensed; and they vented their displeasure on the offender in the way we have described.

A correspondent from County Wexford, who desires to have his name suppressed, writes as follows: "Less than ten miles from the town of ——, Co. Wexford, lives a small farmer named M—, who by dint of thrift and industry has reared a large family decently and comfortably.

"Some twenty years ago Mr. M—, through the death of a relative, fell in for a legacy of about a hundred pounds. As he was already in rather prosperous circumstances, and as his old thatched dwellinghouse was not large enough to accommodate his increasing family, he resolved to spend the money in building a new one.

"Not long afterwards building operations commenced, and in about a year he had a fine slated cottage, or small farm-house, erected and ready for occupation: so far very well; but it is little our friend M— anticipated the troubles which were still ahead of him. He purchased some new furniture at the nearest town, and on a certain day he removed all the furniture which the old house contained into the new one; and in the evening the family found themselves installed in the latter for good, as they thought. They all retired to rest at their usual hour; scarcely were they snugly settled in bed when they heard peculiar noises inside the house. As time passed the din became terrible—there was shuffling of feet, slamming of doors, pulling about of furniture, and so forth. The man of the house got up to explore, but could see nothing, neither was anything disturbed. The door was securely locked as he had left it. After a thorough investigation, in which his wife assisted, he had to own he could find no clue to the cause of the disturbance. The couple went to bed again, and almost immediately the racket recommenced, and continued more or less till dawn.

"The inmates were puzzled and frightened, but determined to try whether the noise would be repeated the next night before telling their neighbours what had happened. But the pandemonium experienced the first night of their occupation was as nothing compared with what they had to endure the second night and for several succeeding nights. Sleep was impossible, and finally Mr.

M— and family in terror abandoned their new home, and retook possession of their old one.

"That is the state of things to this day. The old house has been repaired and is tenanted. The new house, a few perches off, facing the public road, is used as a store-house. The writer has seen it scores of times, and its story is well known all over the country-side. Mr. M— is disinclined to discuss the matter or to answer questions; but it is said he made several subsequent attempts to occupy the house, but always failed to stand his ground when night came with its usual rowdy disturbances.

"It is said that when building operations were about to begin, a little man of bizarre appearance accosted Mr. M— and exhorted him to build on a different site; otherwise the consequences would be unpleasant for him and his; while the local peasantry allege that the house was built across a fairy pathway between two *raths* and that this was the cause of the trouble. It is quite true that there are two large *raths* in the vicinity, and the haunted house is directly in a bee-line between them. For myself I offer no explanation; but I guarantee the substantial accuracy of what I have stated above."

Professor Barrett, in the paper to which we have already referred, draws certain conclusions from his study of this subject; one of the chief of these is that "the widespread belief in fairies, pixies, gnomes, brownies, &c., probably rests on the varied manifestations of poltergeists." The popular explanation of the above story bears out this conclusion, and it is further emphasized by the following, which comes from Portarlington: A man near that town had saved five hundred pounds, and determined to build a house with the money. He fixed on a certain spot, and began to build, very much against the advice of his friends, who said it was on a fairy path, and would bring him ill-luck. Soon the house was finished, and the owner moved in; but the very first night his troubles began, for some unseen hand threw the furniture about and broke it, while the man himself was injured. Being unwilling to lose the value of his money, he tried to make the best of things. But night after night the disturbances continued, and life in the house was impossible; the owner chose the better part of valour and left. No tenant has been found since, and the house stands empty, a silent testimony to the power of the poltergeist.

That versatile writer "Dr. Mick" contributed a poltergeistic experience of his own to the *Tipperary Star*, which, through the courtesy of the editor, we are enabled to reproduce here.

"I do not believe in ghosts or fairies, I do not believe they exist, but yet I cannot get away from an experience of my own, a reality, which, though strange, is true. To corroborate my words I will give the names and addresses of the persons concerned.

"The village of Scotchfort lies about four miles to the south of Ballina, and herein reside an aunt and uncle of the subscriber on a farm by the shores of Lough Conn, purchased some thirty-eight years ago. There was a thatched cottage on the farm, and, previous to my uncle purchasing it, it was owned by Cawleys, a family comprising eight daughters, all of whom died in the house inside two years. Each in turn started to pine, and after lingering for a couple of months passed away.

"Immediately the last one had crossed the bourne, the father, dejected, downcast, almost demented at the calamity that had befallen his family, sold the place, and the consensus of opinion all over the parish was that the 'good people took away the Cawley family.'

"This belief was strengthened by the fact that the house is surrounded by six forts, and my own experience leads me to believe the house was haunted, whatever 'haunted' means. My uncle and aunt, however, got into possession, and it was then that the fun appeared to commence. Night after night when the family retired from work, washing, cooking, etc., commenced, slamming of doors, cleaning of pots, pans, and other utensils. Nobody in the house could sleep, nor could anybody fathom the uncanny happenings. Every morning the kitchen was scrupulously clean or wretchedly dirty, in whichever condition it was left the previous night.

"My grandmother, who has long since gone to her reward, several times rose and went to see what was going on or who were the performing artistes, but except on a few occasions to see figures spectre-like moving about she succeeded in making no further revelation. This I often heard her say, and at this stage of life I will refrain from doing injustice to the dear departed.

"I once went on holidays to this haunted or enchanted region, decide on the appellation yourself, but my stay was cut short, and the following morning with bag and baggage I was bidding 'day-day' to the scene and surroundings, and I did not go back since, nor have I now the slightest inclination to do so. When you hear you may convict me of romancing, but I am not, and the subsequent vacation of the house will go to prove my statements.

"I had heard something about the noises and ructions that used to rattle the house at night after the family retiring, but to be candid, I did not believe a word of it. I went to bed and had not long to wait until the nightly racket started. Such walloping around the kitchen, firing and breaking of delft, slamming of doors, knocking of pots and pans together, I never heard before. I was sleeping with a first cousin named Hegarty, and the first ghoulish gunnery about one o'clock almost turned me inside out! I momentarily expected some dreadful Fee Faw Fum to pull me out of bed!

"I wondered if it was in the 'jigs' or 'rats' or what I was, and at once gave a nudge to Hegarty. 'Ah! Go and sleep, man,' said he, 'they're just commencing now!'

" 'Sleep'! Instantaneous death from fright was more like it! Shaking like an aspen leaf, I was not the size of a threepenny bit under the blanket, perspiring freely, with the crop on my cranium standing erect as the hair in a toothbrush. I prayed and prayed, in fact I recited all the prayers from the Key of Heaven down to Butler's penny-sized Catechism, while wallop after wallop in the kitchen made syllables and semi-syllables of the words on my tongue stagger like a drunken man. I thought I would wake up dead.

"After three hours also there was a cessation of hostilities, and Hegarty, who had been snoring the whole time, turned over on his side, yawned, and after listening a moment remarked, 'They must be gone.' I tried to help him with 'The devil go along with them,' but my organs of speech failed me. Next morning the kitchen was the same as it had been left the previous night.

"Mass was offered up several times in this house by my uncle, Rev. Canon E. Timlin, P.P., and other clergymen, but nothing seemed capable of silencing the noise, and at his dictation, and party at his cost, my aunt decided to leave the place and on another farm erect their present residence at great expense. The old house is now down, and it is a known fact that no person in the neighbourhood or district will go near it, or into the yard after eight or nine o'clock at night."

V

HAUNTED PLACES

THAT houses are haunted and apparitions frequently seen therein are pretty well established facts. The preceding chapters have dealt with this aspect of the subject, and, in view of the weight of evidence to prove the truth of the stories told in them, it would be hard for anyone to doubt that there is such a thing as a haunted house, whatever explanation maybe given of "haunting." We now turn to another division of the subject—the outdoor ghost who haunts the roadways, country lanes, and other places. Sceptics on ghostly phenomena are generally pretty full of explanations when they are told of a ghost having been seen in a particular spot, and the teller may be put down as hyper-imaginative, or as having been deluded by moonlight playing through the trees; while cases are not wanting where a reputation for temperance has been lost by a man telling his experiences of a ghost he happens to have met along some country lane; and the fact that there are cases where an imaginative and nervous person has mistaken for a ghost a white goat or a sheet hanging on a bush only strengthens the sceptic's disbelief and makes him blind to the very large weight of evidence that can be arrayed against him. Some day, no doubt, psychologists and scientists will be able to give us a complete and satisfactory explanation of these abnormal apparitions, but at present we are very much in the dark, and any explanation that may be put forward is necessarily of a tentative nature.

The following story is sent us by Mr. J. J. Crowley, of the Munster and Leinster Bank, who writes as follows: "The scene is outside Clonmel, on the main road leading up to a nice old residence on the side of the mountains called —— Lodge. I happened to be visiting my friends, two other bank men. It was night, about eight o'clock, moonless, and tolerably dark, and when within a quarter of a mile or perhaps less of a bridge over a small stream near the house I saw a girl, dressed in white, wearing a black sash and long flowing hair, walk in the direction from me up the culvert of the bridge and disappear down the other side. At the time I saw it I thought it most peculiar that I could distinguish a figure so far away, and thought a light of some sort must be falling on the girl, or that there were some people about and that some of them had struck a match. When I got to the place I looked about, but could find no person there.

"I related this story to my friends some time after arriving, and was then told that one of them had wakened up in his sleep a few nights previously, and had seen an identical figure standing at the foot of his bed, and rushed in fright from his room, taking refuge for the night with the other lodger. They told the story to their landlady, and learned from her that this apparition had frequently been seen about the place, and was the spirit of one of her daughters who had died years previously rather young, and who, previous to her death, had gone about just as we described the figure we had seen. I had heard nothing of this story until after I had seen the ghost, and consequently it could not be put down to hallucination or over-imagination on my part."

The experiences of two constables of the Royal Irish Constabulary while on despatch duty one winter's night in the early eighties has been sent us by one of the men concerned, and provides interesting reading. It was a fine moonlight night, with a touch of frost in the air, when these two men set out to march the five miles to the next barrack. Brisk walking soon brought them near their destination. The barrack which they were approaching was on the left side of the road, and facing it on the other side was a white-thorn hedge. The road at this point was wide, and as the two constables got within fifty yards of the barrack, they saw a policeman step out from this hedge and move across the road, looking towards the two men as he did so. He was plainly visible to them both. "He was bare-headed" (runs the account), "with his tunic opened down the front, a stout-built man, black-haired, pale, full face, and short mutton-chop whiskers." They thought he was a newly-joined constable who was doing "guard" and had come out to get some fresh air while waiting for a patrol to return. As the two men approached, he disappeared into the shadow of the barrack, and apparently went in by the door; to their amazement, when they came up they found the door closed and bolted, and it was only after loud knocking that they got a sleepy "All right" from someone inside, and after the usual challenging were admitted. There was no sign of the strange policeman when they got in, and on inquiry they learnt that no new constable had joined the station. The two men realised then that they had seen a ghost, but refrained from saying anything about it to the men at the station—a very sensible precaution, considering the loneliness of the average policeman's life in this country.

Some years afterwards the narrator of the above story learnt that a policeman had been lost in a snow-drift near this particular barrack. Whether this be the explanation we leave to others: the facts as stated are well vouched for. There is no evidence to support the theory of hallucination, for the apparition was so vivid that the idea of its being other than normal never entered the constables' heads *till they had got into the barrack*. When they found the door shut and bolted, their amazement was caused by indignation against an apparently unsociable or thoughtless comrade, and it was only afterwards, while discussing the whole thing on their homeward journey, that it occurred to them that it would have been impossible for any ordinary mortal to shut, bolt, and bar a door without making a sound.

In the winter of 1840–1, in the days when snow and ice and all their attendant pleasures were more often in evidence than in these degenerate days, a skating party was enjoying itself on the pond in the grounds of the Castle near Rathfarnham, Co. Dublin. Among the skaters was a man who had with him a very fine curly-coated retriever dog. The pond was thronged with people enjoying themselves, when suddenly the ice gave way beneath him, and the man fell into the water; the dog went to his rescue, and both were drowned. A monument was erected to perpetuate the memory of the dog's heroic self-sacrifice, but only the pedestal now remains. The ghost of the dog is said to haunt the grounds and the public road between the castle gate and the Dodder Bridge. Many people have seen the phantom dog, and the story is well known locally.

The ghost of a boy who was murdered by a Romany is said to haunt one of the lodge gates of the Castle demesne, and the lodge-keeper states that he saw it only a short time ago. The Castle, however, is now in possession of Jesuit Fathers, and the Superior assures us that there has been no sign of a ghost for a long time, his explanation being that the place is so crowded out with new buildings "that even a ghost would have some difficulty in finding a comfortable corner."

It is a fairly general belief amongst students of supernatural phenomena that animals have the psychic faculty developed to a greater extent than we have. There are numerous stories which tell of animals being scared and frightened by something that is invisible to a human being, and the explanation given is that the animal has seen a ghost which we cannot see. A story that is told of a certain spot near the village of G—, in Co. Kilkenny, supports this theory. The account was sent us by the eye-witness of what occurred, and runs as follows: "I was out for a walk one evening near the town of G— about 8.45 P.M., and was crossing the bridge that leads into the S. Carlow district with a small wire-haired terrier dog. When we were about three-quarters of a mile out, the dog began to bark and yelp in a most vicious manner at 'nothing' on the left-hand side of the roadway and near to a straggling hedge. I felt a bit creepy and that something was wrong. The dog kept on barking, but I could at first see nothing, but on looking closely for a few seconds I believe I saw a small grey-white object vanish gradually and noiselessly into the hedge. No sooner had it vanished than the dog ceased barking, wagged his tail, and seemed pleased with his successful efforts." The narrator goes on to say that he made inquiries when he got home, and found that this spot on the road had a very bad reputation, as people had frequently seen a ghost there, while horses had often to be beaten, coaxed, or led past the place. The explanation locally current is that a suicide was buried at the cross-roads near at hand, or that it may be the ghost of a man who is known to have been killed at the spot.

Miss C. Dysart, of Moville, Co. Donegal, contributes another tale illustrative of the psychic power of animals.

"Some years ago, before the War, a friend asked me to take care of her pet dog, and Irish terrier, for some months. Like all of his breed he was a plucky animal, and apparently afraid of nothing.

"One evening, on coming out of my room, I found him

standing on the landing looking down the stairs, growling and with all his bristles erect. He followed me down, and, while I went to get a light, stood at the bottom looking up the stairs, apparently being in a great state of fright. I called him as I went up again; he came up a few steps, then stopped, and refused to move, but stood looking up at the wall at the corner of the stairs, growling all the time.

"I scolded him, and he came on slowly, still keeping his eyes fixed on whatever it was he saw. When he came to the turn of the stairs he crouched against the banisters, growling and showing his teeth, then made a sudden bolt up to the top, where he stood shaking with terror. I tried to make him come down again, but, although usually most obedient, he refused utterly. Thereupon I picked him up, and carried him down the stairs past the place he was afraid of. Then I went up and stood at the spot myself, and called him to come to me. He crawled up slowly, and on reaching me again looked up at the wall, and bolted past. An hour or so afterwards I took him to the head of the stairs. He went up and down and looked all around, seemed quite satisfied that nothing was there, and trotted up and down quite unconcernedly.

"I myself neither saw nor felt anything that evening; but some years before, I distinctly felt someone pass me on those stairs, and remember instinctively standing to one side, although there was nothing to be seen."

The following story has been sent us by the Rev. H. R. B. Gillespie, to whom it was told by one of the witnesses of the incidents described therein. One bright moonlight night some time ago a party consisting of a man, his two daughters, and a friend were driving along a country road in County Leitrim. They came to a steep hill, and all except the driver got down to walk.

One of the two sisters walked on in front, and after her came the other two, followed closely by the trap. They had not gone far, when those in rear saw a shabbily-dressed man walking beside the girl who was leading. But she did not seem to be taking any notice of him, and, wondering what he could be, they hastened to overtake her. But just when they were catching her up the figure suddenly dashed into the shadow of a disused forge, which stood by the side of the road, and as it did so the horse, which up to this had been perfectly quiet, reared up and became unmanageable. The girl beside whom the figure had walked had seen and heard nothing. The road was not bordered by trees or a high hedge, so that it could not have been some trick of the moonlight. One of the girls described the appearance of the figure to a local workman, who said, "It is very like a tinker who was found dead in that forge about six months ago."

Here is another story of a haunted spot on a road, where a "ghost" was seen, not at the witching hour of night, not when evening shadows lengthen, but in broad daylight. It is sent to us by the percipient, a lady, who does not desire to have her name mentioned. She was walking along a country road in the vicinity of Cork one afternoon, and passed various people. She then saw coming towards her a country-woman dressed in an old-fashioned style. This figure approached her, and when it drew near, suddenly staggered, as if under the influence of drink, and disappeared! She hastened to the spot, but searched in vain for any clue to the mystery; the road was bounded by high walls, and there was no gateway or gap through which the figure might slip. Much mystified, she continued on her way, and arrived at her destination. She there mentioned what had occurred, and was then informed by an old resident in the neighbourhood that that woman had constantly been seen up to twenty years before, but not since that date. By the country-people the road was believed to be haunted, but the percipient did not know this at the time.

Mr F. R. B. Kennedy, of Birr, sends the following account of a very curious experience that befell him, and we think our readers will agree with him that it was not his shadow which he beheld! It is interesting to note that this brother was affected too by the presence of the apparition, although he actually saw nothing.

"The following incident happened on a fine moonlight night early in the month of November. My brother Louis and I were out shooting wild duck as they came in flights from the Shannon to the flooded callows adjoining.

"Louis took up a position about four hundred yards away from where I was standing, and we had arranged that when the flight was over that one of us would strike a match to indicate that it was time to go home. In due course Louis struck a match, and I proceeded in his direction. In order to do so I had to cross field with bushes growing here and there through it. The moon was shining and I could see the bushes quite distinctly.

"When I was in the middle of this field I saw what I thought at first was our dog 'Roscoe' coming towards me. I called him, and as I did so, the 'dog' seemed to take the shape of a man or a woman, I could not distinguish which. Then I thought it must be an old man, Willie Dwyer, who was in the habit of shooting duck at night, so I saluted him, calling out, 'Good-night, Willie!' As I stood to speak the figure also stood. I then walked towards the figure to see who it was, but as I moved the figure moved before me. I then ran after it, but it moved before me with equal quickness. Now I commenced to experience a queer creepy sensation. I could feel my hair standing up, and I was thoroughly frightened. So I put the best face I could on the matter. I began to whistle a tune, in order to show that I was not afraid, and turned back in the direction of my brother.

"As I began to move the figure came along beside me, keeping about twenty yards to my right. I could see it distinctly as it passed the bushes. So I challenged it again, saying, 'Who are you?' but I got no reply. At this juncture I seem to have lost my head, for I ran again after the figure, shouting out, 'Stand, or I will fire!' Receiving no response I halted to take aim, the figure also halted, and I aimed my gun at where I thought the legs should be, and fired.

"After this I must have fainted, for the next thing I remember was my brother lifting me up and inquiring what was the matter. He told me afterwards that when he came out to me he experienced a creepy sensation. Some people, to whom I related my adventure, scoffed at the idea of a ghost, and said that it must have been my shadow. This explanation may be discredited, as no shadow is thrown as a separate appearance twenty yards away, and even supposing it to have been a shadow, how is it that it disappeared after I fired? I subsequently learnt that a woman was murdered about fifty years ago near the scene of my adventure."

The following was sent us by Mr. T. J. Westropp, and has points of its own which are interesting; he states: "On the road from Bray to Windgates, at the Deerpark of Kilruddy, is a spot which, whatever be the explanation, is distinguished by weird sounds and (some say) sights. I on one occasion was walking with a friend to catch the train at Bray about eleven o'clock one evening some twenty-five years ago, when we both heard heavy steps and rustling of bracken in the Deerpark; apparently someone got over the gate, crossed the road with heavy steps and fell from the wall next Bray Head, rustling and slightly groaning. The night was lightsome, though without actual moonlight, and we could see nothing over the wall where we had heard the noise.

"For several years after I dismissed the matter as a delusion; but when I told the story to some cousins, they said that another relative (now a Fellow of Trinity College, Dublin) had heard it too, and that there was a local belief that it was the ghost of a poacher mortally wounded by gamekeepers, who escaped across the road and died beyond it." Mr. Westropp afterwards got the relative mentioned above to tell his experience, and it corresponded with his own, except that the ghost was visible. "The clergyman who was rector of Greystones at that time used to say that he had heard exactly similar noises though he had seen nothing."

The following story of an occurrence near Dublin is sent us by a lady who is a very firm believer in ghosts. On a fine night some years ago two sisters were returning home from the theatre. They were walking along a very lonely part of the Kimmage Road about two miles beyond the tram terminus, and were chatting gaily as they went, when suddenly they heard the "clink, clink" of a chain coming towards them. At first they thought it was a goat or a donkey which had got loose, and was dragging its chain along the ground. But they could see nothing, and could hear no noise but the clink of the chain, although the road was clear and straight. Nearer and nearer came the noise, gradually getting louder, and as it passed them closely they distinctly felt a blast or whiff of air. They were paralysed with an indefinable fear, and were scarcely able to drag themselves along the remaining quarter of a mile to their house. The elder of the two was in very bad health, and the other had almost to carry her. Immediately she entered the house she collapsed, and had to be revived with brandy.

An old woman, it seems, had been murdered for her savings by a tramp near the spot where this strange occurrence took place, and it is thought that there is a connection between the crime and the haunting of this part of the Kimmage Road. Whatever the explanation may be, the whole story bears every evidence of truth, and it would be hard for anyone to disprove it.

Churchyards are generally considered to be the hunting-ground of all sorts and conditions of ghosts. People who would on all other occasions, when the necessity arises, prove themselves to be possessed of at any rate a normal amount of courage, turn pale and shiver at the thought of having to pass through a churchyard at dead of night. It may be some encouragement to such to state that out of a fairly large collection of accounts of haunted places, only one relates to a churchyard. The story is told by Mr. G. H. Millar of Edgeworthstown: "During the winter of 1875," he writes, "I attended a soirée about five miles from here. I was riding, and on my way home about 11.30 P.M. I had to pass by the old ruins and burial-ground of Abbeyshrule. The road led round by two sides of the churchyard. It was a bright moonlight night, and as my girth broke I was walking the horse quite slowly. As I passed the ruin, I saw what I took to be a policeman in a long overcoat; he was walking from the centre of the churchyard towards the corner, and, as far as I could see, would be at the corner by the time I would reach it, and we would meet. Quite suddenly, however, he disappeared, and I could see no trace of him. Soon after I overtook a man who had left the meeting long before me. I expressed wonder that he had not been farther on, and he explained that he went a 'round-about' way to avoid passing the old abbey, as he did not want to see 'The Monk.' On questioning him, he told me that a monk was often seen in the churchyard."

A story told of a ghost which haunts a certain spot on an estate near the city of Waterford, bears a certain resemblance to the last story for the reason that it was only after the encounter had taken place in both cases that it was known that anything out of the ordinary had been seen. In the early eighties of last century ——

Court, near Waterford, was occupied by Mr. and Mrs. S— and their family of two young boys and a girl of twenty-one years of age. Below the house is a marshy glen with a big open drain cut through it. Late one evening the daughter was out shooting rabbits near this drain and saw, as she thought, her half-brother standing by the drain in a sailor suit, which like other small boys he wore. She called to him once or twice, and to her surprise got no reply. She went towards him, and when she got close he suddenly disappeared. The next day she asked an old dependent, who had lived many years in the place, if there was anything curious about the glen. He replied at once: "Oh! You mean the little sailor man. Sure, he won't do you any harm." This was the first she had heard of anything of the sort, but it was then found that none of the country-people would go through the glen after dusk.

Some time afterwards two sons of the clergyman of the parish in which —— Court stands were out one evening fishing in the drain, when one of them suddenly said, "What's that sailor doing there?" The other saw nothing, and presently the figure vanished. At the time of the appearance neither had heard of Miss S—'s experience, and no one has been able to explain it, as there is apparently no tradition of any "little sailor man" having been there in the flesh.

Mr. Joseph M'Crossan, a journalist on the staff of the *Strabane Chronicle,* has sent us a cutting from that paper describing a ghost which appeared to men working in an engine-house at Strabane railway station on two successive nights in October 1913. The article depicts very graphically the antics of the ghost and the fear of the men who saw it. Mr. M'Crossan interviewed one of these men (Pinkerton by name), and the story as told in his words is as follows: "Michael Madden, Fred Oliphant, and I were engaged inside a shed cleaning engines, when, at half-past twelve (midnight), a knocking came to all the doors, and continued without interruption, accompanied by unearthly yells. The three of us went to one of the doors, and saw—I could swear to it without doubt—the form of a man of heavy build. I thought I was about to faint. My hair stood high on my head. We all squealed for help, when the watchman and signalman came fast to our aid. Armed with a crowbar, the signalman made a dash at the 'spirit,' but was unable to strike down the ghost, which hovered about our shed till half-past two. It was moonlight, and we saw it plainly. There was no imagination on our part. We three cleaners climbed up the engine, and hid on the roof of the engine, lying there till morning at our wit's end. The next night it came at half-past one. Oliphant approached the spirit within two yards, but he then collapsed, the ghost uttering terrible yells. I commenced work, but the spirit 'gazed' into my face, and I fell forward against the engine. Seven of us saw the ghost this time. Our clothes and everything in the shed were tossed and thrown about."

The other engine-cleaners were interviewed and corroborated Pinkerton's account. One of them stated that he saw the ghost run up and down a ladder leading to a water tank and disappear into it, while the signalman described how he struck at the ghost with a crowbar, but the weapon seemed to go through it. The spirit finally took his departure through the window.

The details of this affair are very much on the lines of the good old-fashioned ghost yarns. But it is hard to see how so many men could labour under the same delusion. The suggestion that the whole thing was a practical joke may also be dismissed, for if the apparition had flesh and bones the crowbar would have soon proved it. The story goes that a man was murdered near the spot some time ago; whether there is any connection between this crime and the apparition it would be hard to say.

However, we are not concerned with explanations (for who, as yet, can explain the supernatural?); the facts as stated have all the appearance of truth.

Mr. Patrick Ryan, of P—, Co. Limerick, gives us two stories as he heard them related by Mr. Michael O'Dwyer of the same place. The former is evidently a very strong believer in supernatural phenomena, but he realises how strong is the unbelief of many, and in support of his stories he gives names of several persons who will vouch for the truth of them. With a few alterations, we give the story in his own words: "Mr. O'Dwyer has related how one night, after he had carried the mails to the train, he went with some fodder for a heifer in a field close to the railway station near to which was a creamery. He discovered the animal grazing near the creamery although how she came to be there was a mystery, as a broad trench separated it from the rest of the field, which is only spanned by a plank used by pedestrians when crossing the field. 'Perhaps,' he said in explanation, 'it was that he should go there to hear.' It was about a quarter to twelve (midnight), and, having searched the field in vain, he was returning home, when, as he crossed the plank, he espied the heifer browsing peacefully in the aforementioned part of the field which was near the creamery. He gave her the fodder and— Heavens! Was he suffering from delusions? Surely his ears were not deceiving him—from the creamery funnel there arose a dense volume of smoke mingled with the sharp hissing of steam and the rattling of cans, all as if the creamery were working, and it were broad daylight. His heifer became startled and bellowed frantically. O'Dwyer, himself a man of nerves, yet possessing all the superstitions of the Celt, was startled and ran without ceasing to his home near by, where he went quickly to bed.

"O'Dwyer is not the only one who has seen this, as I have been told by several of my friends how they heard it. Who knows the mystery surrounding this affair!"

The second story relates to a certain railway station in the south of Ireland; again we use Mr. Ryan's own words: "A near relative of mine" (he writes) "once had occasion to go to the mail train to meet a friend. While sitting talking to O'Dwyer, whom he met on the platform, he heard talking going on in the waiting-room. O'Dwyer heard it also, and they went to the door, but saw nothing save for the light of a waning moon which filtered in through the window. Uncertain, they struck matches, but saw nothing. Again they sat outside, and again they heard the talking, and this time they did not go to look, for they knew about it. In the memory of the writer a certain unfortunate person committed suicide on the railway, and was carried to the waiting-room pending an inquest. He lay all night there till the inquest was held next day. 'Let us not look further into the matter,' said O'Dwyer, and my relative having acquiesced, he breathed a shuddering prayer for the repose of the dead."

The following story, which has been sent as a personal experience by Mr. William Mackey of Strabane, is similar in many ways to an extraordinary case of retro-cognitive vision which occurred some years ago to two English ladies who were paying a visit to Versailles; and who published their experiences in a book entitled, *An Adventure* (London, 1911). Mr. Mackey writes: "It was during the severe winter of the Crimean War, when indulging in my favourite sport of wild-fowl shooting, that I witnessed the following strange scene. It was a bitterly cold night towards the end of November or beginning of December; the silvery moon had sunk in the west shortly before midnight; the sport had been all that could be desired, when I began to realise that the blood was frozen in my veins, and I was on the point of starting for home, when my attention was drawn to the barking of a dog close by, which was followed in a few seconds by the loud report of a musket, the echo of which had scarcely died away in the silent night, when several musket-shots went off in quick succession; this seemed to be the signal for a regular fusillade of musketry, and it was quite evident from the nature of the firing that there was attack and defence.

" For the life of me I could not understand what it all meant; not being superstitious I did not for a moment imagine it was supernatural, notwithstanding that my courageous dog was crouching in abject terror between my legs; beads of perspiration began to trickle down from my forehead, when suddenly there arose a flame as if a house were on fire, but I knew from the position of the blaze (which was only a few hundred yards from where I stood), that there was no house there, or any combustible that would burn, and what perplexed me most was to see pieces of burning thatch and timber sparks fall hissing into the water at my feet. When the fire seemed at its height the firing appeared to weaken, and when the clear sound of a bugle floated out on the midnight air, it suddenly ceased, and I could hear distinctly the sound of cavalry coming at a canter, their accoutrements jingling quite plainly on the frosty air; in a very short time they arrived at the scene of the fight. I thought it an eternity until they took their departure, which they did at the walk.

"It is needless to say that, although the scene of this tumult was on my nearest way home, I did not venture that way, as, although there are many people who would say that I never knew what fear was, I must confess on this occasion I was thoroughly frightened.

"At breakfast I got a good sound rating from my father for staying out so late. My excuse was that I fell asleep and had a horrible dream, which I related. When I finished I was told I had been dreaming with my eyes open!—that I was not the first person who had witnessed this strange sight. He then told me the following narrative: 'It was towards the end of the seventeenth century that a widow named Sally Mackey and her three sons lived on the outskirts of the little settlement of the Mackeys. A warrant was issued by the Government against the three sons for high treason, the warrant being delivered for execution to the officer in command of the infantry regiment stationed at Lifford. A company was told off for the purpose of effecting the arrest, and the troops set out from Lifford at 11 P.M.

"'The cottage home of the Mackeys was approached by a bridle-path, leading from the main road to Derry, which only permitted the military to approach in single file; they arrived there at midnight, and the first intimation the inmates had of danger was the barking, and then the shooting, of the collie dog. Possessing as they did several stand of arms, they opened fire on the soldiers as they came in view and killed and wounded several; it was the mother, Sally Mackey, who did the shooting, the sons loading the muskets. Whether the cottage went on fire by accident or design was never known; it was only when the firing from the cottage ceased and the door was forced open that the officer in command rushed in and brought out the prostrate form of the lady, who was severely wounded and burned. All the sons perished, but the soldiers suffered severely, a good many being killed and wounded.

"'The firing was heard by the sentries at Lifford, and a troop of cavalry was despatched to the scene of conflict, but only arrived in time to see the heroine dragged from the burning cottage. She had not, however, been fatally wounded, and lived for many years afterwards with a kinsman. My father remembered conversing with old men, when he was a boy, who remembered her well.

She seemed to take a delight in narrating incidents of the fight to those who came to visit her, and would always finish up by making them feel the pellets between the skin and her ribs.'"

VI

APPARITIONS AT OR AFTER DEATH

IT has been said by a very eminent literary man that the accounts of the appearance of people at or shortly after the moment of death make very dull reading as a general rule. This may be; they are certainly not so lengthy, or full of detail, as the accounts of haunted houses—nor could such be expected. In our humble opinion, however, they are full of interest, and open up problems of telepathy and thought-transference to which the solutions may not be found for years to come. That people have seen the image of a friend or relative at the moment of dissolution, sometimes in the ordinary garb of life, sometimes with symbolical accompaniments, or that they have been made acquainted in some abnormal manner with the fact that such a one has passed away, seems to be demonstrated beyond all reasonable doubt. But we would hasten to add that such appearances are not a proof of existence after death, nor can they be regarded in the light of special interventions of a merciful Providence. Were they either they would surely occur far oftener. The question is, why do they occur at all? As it is, the majority of them seem to happen for no particular reason, and are often seen by persons who have little or no connection with the deceased, not by their nearest and dearest, as one might expect.

It is supposed they are *veridical* hallucinations, *i.e.* ones which correspond with objective events at a distance, and are caused by a telepathic impact conveyed from the mind of an absent agent to the mind of the percipient.

From their nature they fall under different heads. The majority of them occur at what may most conveniently be described as the time of death, though how closely they approximate in reality to the instant of the Great Change it is impossible to say. So we have divided this chapter into three groups:

(1) Appearances at the time of death (as explained above).

(2) Appearances clearly *after* the time of death,

(3) In this third group we hope to give three curious tales of appearances some time *before* death.

GROUP I

We commence this group with stories in which the phenomena connected with the respective deaths were not perceived as representations of the human form. In the first only sounds were heard. It was sent as a personal experience by the late Archdeacon of Limerick, Very Rev. J. A. Haydn, LL.D. "In the year 1879 there lived in the picturesque village of Adare, at a distance of about eight or nine miles from my residence, a District Inspector named ——, with whom I enjoyed a friendship of the most intimate and fraternal kind. At the time I write of, Mrs. —— was expecting the arrival of their third child. She was a particularly tiny and fragile woman, and much anxiety was felt as to the result of the impending event. He and she had very frequently spent pleasant days at my house, with all the apartments of which they were thoroughly acquainted—a fact of importance in this narrative.

"On Wednesday, October 17, 1879, I had a very jubilant letter from my friend, announcing that the expected event had successfully happened on the previous day, and that all was progressing satisfactorily. On the night of the following Wednesday, October 22, I retired to bed at about ten o'clock. My wife, the children, and two maid-servants were all sleeping upstairs, and I had a small bed in my study, which was on the ground floor. The house was shrouded in darkness, and the only sound that broke the silence was the ticking of the hall-clock.

"I was quietly preparing to go to sleep, when I was much surprised at hearing, with the most unquestionable distinctness, the sound of light, hurried footsteps, exactly suggestive of those of an active, restless young female, coming in from the hall door and traversing the hall. They then, apparently with some hesitation, followed the passage leading to the study door, on arriving at which they stopped. I then heard the sound of a light, agitated hand apparently searching for the handle of the door. By this time, being quite sure that my wife had come down and wanted to speak to me, I sat up in bed, and called to her by name, asking what was the matter. As there was no reply, and the sounds had ceased, I struck a match, lighted a candle, and opened the door. No one was visible or audible. I went upstairs, found all the doors shut and everyone asleep. Greatly puzzled, I returned to the study and went to bed, leaving the candle alight. Immediately the whole performance was circumstantially repeated, but *this* time the handle of the door was grasped by the invisible hand, and *partly* turned, then relinquished. I started out of bed and renewed my previous search, with equally futile results. The clock struck eleven, and from that time all disturbances ceased.

"On Friday morning I received a letter stating that Mrs. —— had died at about midnight on the previous Wednesday. I hastened off to Adare and had an interview with my bereaved friend. With one item of our conversation I will close. He told me that his wife sank rapidly on Wednesday, until when night came on she became delirious. She spoke incoherently, as if revisiting scenes and places once familiar. 'She thought she was in *your* house,' he said, 'and was apparently holding a conversation with *you*, as she used to keep silence at intervals as if listening to your replies.' I asked him if he could possibly remember the hour at which the imaginary conversation took place. He replied that, curiously enough, he could tell it accurately, as he had looked at his watch, and found the time between half-past ten and eleven o'clock—the exact time of the mysterious manifestations heard by me."

The daughter of a well-known clergyman in the Diocese of Cork has sent us the following account of sounds at the time of death being heard by two people. She furnished us with some names, but on consideration we have thought it best not to publish them.

"On the morning of Saturday, July 26, 1976, my father went into the study of his Rectory in Co. Cork, and commenced to read. His attention was soon diverted by a constant recurring noise that seemed to be over his head: it sounded like a tapping, or perhaps it would be more accurate to say it resembled the sound made by a ball being dropped from a height—pop, pop, pop!—gradually growing fainter until it died away, and then after a pause, beginning again.

"As a nursery was overhead his study he naturally assumed that it was a noise made by his children, and tried not to notice it, though at the same time he felt curiously upset and restless. About twelve o'clock he could stand it no longer, and went upstairs to where his wife was. On his telling her the reason for his coming she informed him that the children had been out for the entire morning. They went together into the deserted nursery, and listened; she could hear nothing, but he did, and continued to hear it at intervals during the entire day, until it ceased towards the night.

"The cook, who was down in the basement, assured her mistress that he had got a terrible fright that morning, for she had heard a man's voice, which she did not recognise, calling 'Mary! Mary!'

"Shortly after my father heard very sad news, which threw some light on the mysterious occurrence. The former occupant of the house had been made a Bishop some ten years previously. He had fallen ill with fever, and in a moment of delirium had inflicted such injuries upon himself that he died in Dublin the morning the sounds were heard. His wife's name was Mary; his bedroom had been the room over the study, which we used as a nursery, while in the basement he had fitted up a workshop."

We shall now give two stories in which the appearance of light is an indication of the moment of death. The first of these is not a first-hand experience; it was sent to the writer by the Rev. H. R. B. Gillespie, to whom it was told by the percipient.

The eldest brother of a family lived at home most of his life. The youngest brother married, and went out in the world, but subsequently fell into ill-health, and returned with his wife and son to stay with his father. While there he became so ill that for months he was confined to bed, and there was no hope of recovery. Finally he died in the month of July.

On the evening of his death his eldest brother was out walking in the fields accompanied by an old nurse who had been with the members of the family since the time they were children. As the brother drew near the house he noticed what he described as "rays like the rays of the setting sun coming round the corner of the house." From where he was standing he could not see the window of his brother's bedroom; it was in the front of the house, and he was at the side. But his impression was, that the rays came from the window round the corner, and that in the centre of them was a "misty light," which came towards him till it almost reached the earth. He felt very uneasy as the light came nearer and nearer, but when it had almost reached to where he was standing "it shot up like a shooting-star, only going the wrong way."

He said to the nurse, "J. is dead!" and walked on quickly towards the front door, which one of his sisters was just opening in order to go out and look for him. He said to her, "You need not tell me the sad news—I know he has just died!" It was nearly 9.30 PM. The nurse did not see the rays of light at all, and only heard the elder brother say that the sick man had passed away.

A lady sends the following personal experience: "I had a cousin in the country who was not very strong, and on one occasion she desired me to go to her, and accompany her to K——. I consented to do so, and arranged a day to go and meet her: this was in the month of February. The evening before I was to go, I was sitting by the fire in my small parlour about 5 P.M. There was no light in the room except what proceeded from the fire. Beside the fireplace was an armchair, where my cousin usually sat when she was with me. Suddenly that chair was illuminated by a light so intensely bright that it actually seemed to *heave* under it, though the remainder of the room remained in semi-darkness. I called out in amazement, 'What has happened to the chair?' In a moment the light vanished, and the chair was as before. In the morning I heard that my cousin had died about the same time that I saw the light."

Canon W. F. Johnstone, of Bansha Rectory, Tipperary, sends an account of an appearance at death which was told to him by his father, the late St. George Johnstone. It marks a transition stage between the stories that precede and follow it in this chapter.

"Many years ago, when I was quite a small boy, my father, who was a keen astronomer, was out one fine moonlight night in the late autumn indulging in his favourite hobby, when he observed a curious isolated cloud or mist, globular in shape, resting at a distance of about one hundred yards on the broad flatly trimmed hedge which bordered the walk on which he was standing. He was wondering what it might be, when, to his surprise, it began to move slowly along the flat top of the broad hedge as if on a path, until it came to rest within a few yards of him. Then, to his utter amazement, the outlines of a face began to appear in the centre of this circular ball of mist, and gradually developed into the likeness of his mother's countenance, set, as it were in a framework of mist. He saw this face distinctly and for the space of some seconds, when it broke into a smile, and in a moment the vision dissolved. His mother died on the day, and at the very hour, on which the globular mist appeared.

"This is, as far as my memory serves me—and the story made a deep impression upon me at the time—the exact account given me by my father years after it took place. I believe it to be true in every particular. My father was a cultured, highly educated man, intensely practical, and not at all a dreamer of dreams."

The following story is sent by Mr. F. C. Pilkington:

In the year of the dreadful cholera a certain County family, who are still well known there, resided in Clare. When the plague was at its worst the female members of this family were sent for greater safety to a remote part of the County, where they had a summer residence, at which they were wont to spend some months every year.

There were either four or five sisters, one of whom was the

writer's grandmother. A brother was a doctor practising in Dublin, and he came to Ennis in the hope of being able to give some medical assistance to the sufferers. The people were dying in hundreds, and the local doctors were terribly overworked and unable to cope with the ravages of the dread disease.

The sisters learned that their brother (Charles was his name) had arrived in Ennis, and they looked forward to a visit from him before he returned to Dublin.

One night they all felt strangely uneasy, and were possessed with that peculiar sense of impending evil which most people must have experienced at one time or another. One of the sisters decided she would go upstairs and lie down, but the others preferred to remain up, so pulled their chairs round the fire and prepared for an all-night sitting.

Presently they heard the front gate open and the sound of a horse's hoofs galloping on the short drive from the public road to the house. They all stood up to go to the door, and in the hall met the sister who had gone to lie down and who had also heard the horse. The same idea occurred to each at once, that it was Charles, who had written from Ennis to pay them a surprise visit.

The horse could now be heard almost at the door, which the sisters flung open with a cry of welcome on their lips. When the door was opened there was nothing to be seen or heard. Dead silence reigned. Terror-stricken now they closed the door and returned to the sitting-room. The clock on the mantelpiece showed the time to be 12.30, and, as sleep for any of them was now more impossible than ever, they huddled together over the fire during the dreary hours before the dawn of day.

At long last dawn came, and with it a messenger who had written on horseback from Ennis.

This was the message which the sisters read in the light of the early dawn: "Charles died at 12.30 this morning." He had fallen a victim to the plague.

We now come to the ordinary type, *i.e.* where a figure appears. The following tale illustrates a point we have already alluded to, namely, that the apparition is sometimes seen by a disinterested person, and not by those whom one would naturally expect should see it. A lady writes as follows: "At Island Magee is the Knowehead Lonan, a long, hilly, narrow road, bordered on either side by high thorn-hedges and fields. Twenty years ago, when I was a young girl, I used to go to the post-office at the Knowehead on Sunday mornings down the Lonan, taking the dogs for the run. One Sunday as I had got to the top of the hill on my return journey, I looked back, and saw a man walking rapidly after me, but still a good way off. I hastened my steps, for the day was muddy, and I did not want him to see me in a bedraggled state. But he seemed to come on so fast as to be soon close behind me, and I wondered he did not pass me, so on we went, I never turning to look back. About a quarter of a mile farther on I met A. B. on 'Dick's Brae,' on her way to church or Sunday school, and stopped to speak to her. I wanted to ask who the man was, but he seemed to be so close that I did not like to do so, and expected he had passed. When I moved on, I was surprised to find he was still following me, while my dogs were lagging behind with downcast heads and drooping tails.

"I then passed a cottage where C. D. was out feeding her fowls. I spoke to her, and then feeling that there was no longer anyone behind, looked back, and saw the man standing with her. I would not have paid any attention to the matter had not A. B. been down at our house that afternoon, and I casually asked her:

"'Who was the man who was just behind me when I met you on Dick's Brae?'

"'What man?' said she; and noting my look of utter astonishment, added, 'I give you my word I never met a soul but yourself from the time I left home till I went down to Knowehead Lonan.'

"Next day C. D. came to work for us, and I asked her who was the man who was standing beside her after I passed her on Sunday.

"'Naebody!' she replied, 'I saw naebody but yoursel'.'

"It all seemed very strange, and so they thought too. About three weeks later news came that C. D.'s only brother, a sailor, was washed overboard that Sunday morning."

The following story is not a first-hand experience, but is sent by the gentleman to whom it was related by the percipient. The latter said to him:

"I was sitting in this same chair I am in at present one evening, when I heard a knock at the front door. I went myself to see who was there, and on opening the door saw my old friend P. Q. standing outside with his gun in his hand. I was surprised at seeing him, but asked him to come in and have something. He came inside the porch into the lamplight, and stood there for a few moments; then he muttered something about being sorry he had disturbed me, and that he was on his way to see his brother, Colonel Q., who lived about a mile farther on. Without any further explanation he walked away towards the gate into the dusk.

"I was greatly surprised and perplexed, but as he had gone I sat down again by the fire. About an hour later another knock came to the door, and I again went out to see who was there. On opening it I found P. Q.'s groom holding a horse, and he asked me where he was, as he had missed his way in the dark, and did not know the locality. I told him, and then asked him where he was going, and why, and he replied that his master was dead (at his own house about nine miles away), and that he had been sent to announce the news to Colonel Q."

Canon J. C. Trotter, formerly Incumbent of Ardrahan, sends the following:

"My maternal grandmother lived with my father and mother in Belfast. She was dying, and my mother was sitting up with her. The old woman's hair had become dishevelled through tossing about on her pillow, and in order to get something to keep it tidy my mother went up to a bedroom on a higher floor in which my father (an invalid) was sleeping. She glanced towards his bed, saw that he was asleep, opened a drawer gently, and took out a piece of ribbon with which she tied up her mother's hair.

"Very shortly after this the sick woman passed away. My mother went up immediately to my father's room to acquaint him of the fact. She found him awake, and he at once remarked on her entry:

"'I know what you have come to tell me—mother is gone!'

"'Yes!' replied my mother. 'But how did you know?'

"'I saw her!' was the answer. 'she said "John, I am crossing the Jordan!" I asked, "What is the prospect, mother?" She replied, "Bright! Bright! Bright!" And each time she repeated that word her face grew less distinct. But what struck me as remarkable was, that her hair was confined by a ribbon!'" Canon Trotter adds that his father named the colour of the ribbon, and that it exactly corresponded to the colour of that one with which his mother had tied up the dying woman's hair.

Miss Grene, of Grene Park, Co. Tipperary, relates a story which was told her by the late Miss ——, sister of a former Dean of Cashel. The latter, an old lady, stated that one time she was staying with a friend in a house in the suburbs of Dublin. In front of the house was the usual grass plot, divided into two by a short gravel path which led down to a gate which opened on to the street. She and her friend were one day engaged in needlework in one of the front rooms, when they heard the gate opening, and on looking out the window they saw an elderly gentleman of their acquaintance coming up the path. As he approached the door both exclaimed: "Oh, how good of him to come and see us!" As he was not shown into the sitting-room, one of them rang the bell, and said to the maid when she appeared, "You have not let Mr. So-and-so in; he is at the door for some little time." The maid went to the hall door, and returned to say that there was no one there. Next day they learnt that he had died just at the hour that they had seen him coming up the path.

The following tale contains a curious point. A good many years ago the Rev. Henry Morton, now dead, held a curacy in Ireland. He had to pass through the graveyard when leaving his house to visit the parishioners. One beautiful moonlight night he was sent for to visit a sick person, and was accompanied by his brother, a medical man, who was staying with him. After performing the religious duty they returned through the churchyard, and were chatting about various matters when to their astonishment a figure passed them, both seeing it. This figure left the path, and went in among the gravestones, and then disappeared. They could not understand this at all, so they went to the spot where the disappearance took place, but, needless to say, could find nobody after the most careful search. Next morning they heard that the person visited had died just after their departure, while the most marvellous thing of all was that the burial took place at the very spot where they had seen the phantom disappear.

The Rev. D. B. Knox communicates the following: in a girls' boarding-school several years ago two of the boarders were sleeping in a large double-bedded room with two doors. About two o'clock in the morning the girls were awakened by the entrance of a tall figure in clerical attire, the face of which they did not see. They screamed in fright, but the figure moved in a slow and stately manner past their beds, and out the other door. It also appeared to one or two of the other boarders, and seemed to be looking for someone. At length it reached the bed of one who was evidently known to it. The girl woke up and recognised her father. He did not speak, but gazed for a few moments at his daughter, and then vanished. Next morning a telegram was handed to her which communicated the sad news that her father had died on the previous evening at the hour when he appeared to her.

Here is a story of a very old type. It occurred a good many years ago. A gentleman named Miller resided in Co. Wexford, while his friend and former schoolfellow lived in the North of Ireland. This long friendship led them to visit at each other's houses from time to time, but for Mr. Miller there was a deep shadow of sorrow over these otherwise happy moments, for, while he enjoyed the most enlightened religious opinions, his friend was an unbeliever. The last time they were together Mr. Scott said, "My dear friend, let us solemnly promise that whichever of us shall die first shall appear to the other after death, if it be possible." "Let it be so, if God will," replied Mr. Miller. One morning some time after, about three o'clock, the latter was awakened by a brilliant light in his bedroom; he imagined that the house must be on fire, when he felt what seemed to be a hand laid on him, and heard his friend's voice say distinctly, "There is a God, just but terrible in His judgments," and all again was dark. Mr. Miller at once wrote down this remarkable experience. Two days later he received a letter announcing Mr. Scott's death on the night, and at the hour, that he had seen the light in his room.

The above leads us on to the famous "Beresford Ghost," which is generally regarded as holding the same position relative to Irish ghosts that Dame Alice Kyteler used to hold with respect to Irish witches and wizards. The story is so well known, and has been published so often, that only a brief allusion is necessary, with the added information that the best version is to be found in Andrew Lang's *Dreams and Ghosts*, chapter viii. (Silver Library Edition). Lord Tyrone appeared after death one night to Lady Beresford at Gill Hall, in accordance with a promise (as in the last story) made in early life. He assured her that the religion as revealed by Jesus Christ was the only true one (both he and Lady Beresford had been brought up Deists), told her that she was *enceinte* and would bear a son, and also foretold her second marriage, and the time of her death. In proof whereof he drew the bed-hangings through an iron hook, wrote his name in her pocket-book, and finally placed a hand cold as marble on her wrist, at which the sinews shrunk up. To the day of her death Lady Beresford wore a black ribbon round her wrist; this was taken off before her burial, and it was found the nerves were withered, and the sinews shrunken, as she had previously described to her children.

GROUP II

We now come to some stories of apparitions seen some time after the hour of death. The late Canon Ross-Lewin, of Limerick, furnished the following incident in his own family. "My uncle, John Dillon Ross-Lewin, lieutenant in the 30th Regiment, was mortally wounded at Inkerman on November 5, 1854, and died on the morning of the 6th. He appeared that night to his mother, who was then on a visit in Co. Limerick, intimating his death, and indicating where the wound was. The strangest part of the occurrence is, that when news came later on of the casualties at Inkerman, the first account as to the wound did *not* correspond with what the apparition indicated to his mother, but the final account did. Mrs. Ross-Lewin was devoted to her son, and he was equally attached to her; she, as the widow of a field officer who fought at Waterloo, would be able to comprehend the battle scene, and her mind at the time was centred on the events of the Crimean War."

A clergyman, who desires that all names be suppressed, sends the following: "In my wife's father's house a number of female servants were kept, of whom my wife, before she was married, was in charge. On one occasion the cook took ill with appendicitis, and was operated on in the Infirmary, where I attended her as hospital chaplain. She died, however, and was buried by her friends. Some days after the funeral my wife was standing at a table in the kitchen which was so placed that any person standing at it could see into the passage outside the kitchen, if the door happened to be open. [The narrator enclosed a rough plan which made the whole story perfectly clear.] She was standing one day by herself at the table, and the door was open. This was in broad daylight, about eleven o'clock in the morning in the end of February or beginning of March. She was icing a cake, and therefore was hardly thinking of ghosts. Suddenly she looked up from her work, and glanced through the open kitchen door into the passage leading past the servants' parlour into the dairy. She saw quite distinctly the figure of the deceased cook pass towards the dairy; she was dressed in the ordinary costume she used to wear in the mornings, and seemed in every respect quite normal. My wife was not, at the moment, in the least shocked or surprised, but on the contrary she followed, and searched in the dairy, into which she was just in time to see her skirts disappearing. Needless to say, nothing was visible."

Canon Courtenay Moore, M.A., Rector of Mitchelstown, contributes a personal experience. "It was about eighteen years ago—I cannot fix the exact date—that Samuel Penrose returned to this parish from the Argentine. He was getting on so well abroad that he would have remained there, but his wife fell ill, and for her sake he returned to Ireland. He was a carpenter by trade, and his former employer was glad to take him into his service again. Sam was a very respectable man of sincere religious feelings. Soon after his return he met with one or two rather severe accidents, and had a strong impression that a fatal one would happen him before long; and so it came to pass. A scaffolding gave way one day, and precipitated him on to a flagged stone floor. He did not die immediately, but his injuries proved fatal. He died in a Cork hospital soon after his admission: I went to Cork to officiate at his funeral. About noon the next day I was standing at my hall door, and the form of poor Sam, the upper half of it, seemed to pass before me. He looked peaceful and happy—it was a momentary vision, but perfectly distinct. The truncated appearance puzzled me very much, until some time after I read a large book by F. W. H. Myers, in which he made a scientific analysis and induction of such phenomena, and said that they were almost universally seen in this half-length form. I do not profess to explain what I saw: its message, if it had a message, seemed to be that poor Sam was at last at rest and in peace."

A story somewhat similar to the above was related to us, in which the apparition seems certainly to have been sent with a definite purpose. Two maiden ladies, whom we shall call Miss A. X. and Miss B. Y., lived together for a good many years. As one would naturally expect, they were close friends, and had the most intimate relations with each other, both being extremely religious women. In process of time Miss B. Y. died, and after death Miss A. X. formed the impression, for some unknown reason, that all was not well with her friend—that, in fact, her soul was not at rest. This thought caused her great uneasiness and trouble of mind. One day she was sitting in her armchair thinking over this, and crying bitterly. Suddenly she saw in front of her a brilliant light, in the midst of which was her friend's face, easily recognisable, but transfigured, and wearing a most beatific expression. She rushed towards it with her arms outstretched, crying, "Oh! B., why have you come?" At this the apparition faded away, but ever after Miss A. X. was perfectly tranquil in mind with respect to her friend's salvation.

A lady has sent the following experience of her son, in which the latter beheld the apparition of a person who had no connection with him. It may be that the dying man had some vivid thoughts of his old home which were telepathically conveyed across half the globe, and so caused the vision or the dream—whichever we choose to call it.

"One night my son woke up and saw leaning over his bed an old man with a long grey beard. He never mentioned this appearance until the following night when we and some friends were sitting round the fire. Amongst the company was the gentleman who had lived in the house before us. As soon as my son had related his experience that gentleman exclaimed, 'Why, that seems very like old H.! He lived in this house before I came to it, and subsequently went to America.' We thought no more of the matter, but a week later a cable came from America to say that old man had died. It seems very strange, for neither my son nor any of my family had ever seen that old man, and yet my son described him so plainly that people who had known him said it could be none other than he."

This group may be brought to a conclusion by a story sent by Mr. T. MacFadden. It is not a personal experience, but happened to his father, and in an accompanying letter he states that he often heard the latter describe the incidents related therein, and that he certainly saw the ghost.

"The island of Inishinny, which is the scene of this story, is one of the most picturesque islands on the Donegal coast. With the islands of Gola and Inismaan it forms a perfectly natural harbour and safe anchorage for ships during storms. About Christmas some forty or fifty years ago a small sailing-ship put into Gola Roads (as this anchorage is called) during a prolonged storm, and the captain and two men had to obtain provisions from Bunbeg, as, owing to their being detained so long, their supply was almost exhausted. They had previously visited the island on several occasions, and made themselves at home with the people from the mainland who were temporarily resident upon it.

"The old bar at its best was never very safe for navigation, and this evening it was in its element, as with every storm it presented one boiling, seething mass of foam. The inhabitants of the island saw the frail small boat from the ship securely inside the bar, and prophesied some dire calamity should the captain and the two sailors venture to return to the ship that night. But the captain and his companions, having secured sufficient provisions, decided (as far as I can remember the story), even in spite of the entreaties of those on shore, to return to the ship. The storm was increasing, and what with their scanty knowledge of the intricacies of the channel, and the darkness of the night, certain it was the next morning their craft was found washed ashore on the island, and the body of the captain was discovered by the first man who made the round of the shore looking for logs of timber, or other useful articles washed ashore from wrecks. The bodies of the two sailors were never recovered, and word was sent immediately to the captain's wife in Deny, who came in a few days and gave directions for the disposal of her husband's corpse.

"The island was only temporarily inhabited by a few people who had cattle and horses grazing there for some weeks in the year, and after this catastrophe they felt peculiarly lonely, and sought refuge from their thoughts by all spending the evening together in one house. This particular evening they were all seated round the fire having a chat, when they heard steps approaching the door. Though the approach was fine, soft sand, yet the steps were audible as if coming on hard ground. They knew there was no one on the island save the few who were sitting quietly round the fire, and so in eager expectation they faced round to the door. What was their amazement when the door opened, and a tall, broad-shouldered man appeared and filled the whole doorway—and that man the captain who had been buried several days previously. He wore the identical suit in which he had often visited the island and even the "cheese-cutter" cap, so common a feature of sea-faring men's apparel, was not wanting. All were struck dumb with terror, and a woman who sat in a corner opposite the door, exclaimed in Irish in a low voice to my father:

"'O God! Patrick, there's the captain.'

"My father, recovering from the first shock, when he saw feminine courage finding expression in words, said in Irish to the apparition:

"'Come in!'

"They were so certain of the appearance that they addressed him in his own language, as they invariably talked Irish in the district in those days. But no sooner had he uttered the invitation than the figure, without the least word or sign, moved back, and disappeared from their view. They rushed out, but could discover no sign of any living person within the confines of the island. Such is the true account of an accident, by which three men lost their lives, and the ghostly sequel, in which one of them appeared to the eyes of four people, two of whom are yet alive, and can vouch for the accuracy of this narrative."

GROUP III

We now come to the third group of this chapter, in which we shall relate two first-hand experiences of tragedies being actually witnessed some time before they happened, as well as a reliable second-hand story of an apparition being seen two days before the death occurred. The first of these is sent by a lady, the percipient, who desires that her name be suppressed; with it was enclosed a letter from a gentleman who stated that he could testify to the truth of the following facts:

"The morning of May 18, 1902, was one of the worst that ever dawned in Killarney. All through the day a fierce nor'-wester raged, and huge white-crested waves, known locally as 'The O'Donoghue's white horses,' beat on the shores of Lough Leane. Then followed hail-showers such as I have never seen before or since. Hailstones quite as large as small marbles fell with such rapidity, and seemed so hard that the glass in the windows of the room in which I stood appeared to be about to break into fragments every moment. I remained at the window, gazing out on the turbulent waters of the lake. Sometimes a regular fog appeared, caused by the terrible downpour of rain and the fury of the gale.

"During an occasional lull I could see the islands plainly looming in the distance. In one of these clear intervals, the time being about 12.30 P.M., five friends of mine were reading in the room in which I stood. 'Quick! Quick!' I cried. 'Is that a boat turned over?' My friends all ran to the windows, but could see nothing. I persisted, however, and said, 'It is on its side, with the keel turned towards us, and it is empty.' Still none of my friends could see anything. I then ran out, and got one of the men-servants to go down to a gate, about one hundred yards nearer the lake than where I stood. He had a powerful telescope, and remained with great difficulty in the teeth of the storm with his glass for several minutes, but could see nothing. When he returned another man took his place, but he also failed to see anything.

"I seemed so distressed that those around me kept going backwards and forwards to the windows, and then asked me what was the size of the boat I had seen. I gave them the exact size, measuring by landmarks. They then assured me that I must be absolutely wrong, as it was on rare occasions that a 'party' boat, such as the one I described, could venture on the lakes on such a day. Therefore there were seven persons who thought I was wrong in what I had seen. I still contended that I saw the boat, the length of which I described, as plainly as possible.

"The day wore on, and evening came. The incident was apparently more or less forgotten by all but me, until at 8 A.M. on the following morning, when the maid brought up tea, her first words were, 'Ah, miss, is it not terrible about the accident!' Naturally I said, 'What accident, Mary?' She replied, 'There were thirteen people drowned yesterday evening out of a four-oared boat.' That proved that the boat I had seen at 12.30 P.M. was a vision foreshadowing the wreck of the boat off Darby's Garden at 5.30 P.M. The position, shape, and size of the boat seen by me were identical with the one that was lost on the evening of May 18, 1902."

The second story relates how a lady witnessed a vision (shall we call it) of a suicide a week before the terrible deed was committed. This incident surely makes it clear that such cannot be looked upon as special interventions of Providence, for if the lady had recognised the man, she might have prevented his rash act. Mrs. MacAlpine says: "In June 1889, I drove to Castleblaney, in Co. Monaghan, to meet my sister: I expected her at three o'clock, but as she did not come by that train, I put up the horse and went for a walk in the demesne. At length becoming tired, I sat down on a rock by the edge of a lake. My attention was quite taken up with the beauty of the scene before me, as it was a glorious summer's day. Presently I felt a cold chill creep through me, and a curious stiffness came over my limbs, as if I could not move, though wishing to do so. I felt frightened, yet chained to the spot, and as if impelled to stare at the water straight before me. Gradually a black cloud seemed to rise, and in the midst of it I saw a tall man, in a tweed suit, jump into the water, and sink. In a moment the darkness was gone, and I again became sensible of the heat and sunshine, but I was awed, and felt eerie. This happened about June 25, and on July 3 a Mr. ——, a bank clerk, committed suicide by drowning himself in the lake."[10]

The following incident occurred in the United States, but, as it is closely connected with this country, it will not seem out of place to insert it here. It is sent by Mr. Richard Hogan as the personal experience of his sister, Mrs. Mary Murnane, and is given in her own words.

---

[10] *Proceedings S.P.R., x. 332.*

"On the 4th of August 1886, at 10.30 o'clock in the morning, I left my own house, 21 Montrose St., Philadelphia, to do some shopping. I had not proceeded more than fifty yards when on turning the corner of the street I observed my aunt approaching me within five or six yards. I was greatly astonished, for the last letter I had from home (Limerick) stated that she was dying of consumption, but the thought occurred to me that she might have recovered somewhat, and come out to Philadelphia. This opinion was quickly changed as we approached each other, for our eyes met, and she had the colour of one who had risen from the grave. I seemed to feel my hair stand on end, for just as we were about to pass each other she turned her face towards me, and I gasped, 'My God, she is dead, and is going to speak to me!' but no word was spoken, and she passed on. After proceeding a short distance I looked back, and she continued on to Washington Avenue, where she disappeared from me. There was no other person near at the time, and being so close, I was well able to note what she wore. She held a sunshade over her head, and the clothes, hat, &c., were those I knew so well before I left Ireland. I wrote home telling what I had seen, and asking if she was dead. I received a reply saying she was not dead at the date I saw her, but had been asking if a letter had come from me for some days before her death. It was just two days before she actually died that I had seen her."

A gentleman sends the following account of an experience, a premonition of death, which was shared by his friend, and which can hardly be attributed to natural causes.

"The incident I am about to relate occurred in the year 1918 about twenty to one in the morning. It was soft and fine, and not very dark, in fact it was just such a night as one would expect at the period, which was mid-September.

My occupation at this time was that of engine-cleaner, at which

I worked with two comrades in an engine-shed about a quarter of a mile from the local railway station. Our hours of duty were from 7 P.M to 7 A.M, and at the time the incident which I am about to relate occurred I had done three years of this continuous night-work. I mentioned this fact, as it will set aside any suspicion that I might have been in any way 'nervy' of the darkness or anything else; as it happens, the dark night was our actual day! It was my usual custom to go every night for a can of clean water from a pump on the town side of the station. On the left one would pass a public-house, while on the right was a graveyard.

"On this particular night I went for the water as usual, and was accompanied on this errand by a friend, another cleaner. It was, as I have said, about twenty to one. The night was unusually still and quiet, a fact which we remarked to each other in the course of conversation. We went along, and just as we were passing the cemetery a heavy gust of wind, with a mournful wailing sound, suddenly sprang up and seemed to catch us in the back. We stopped dead just outside the graveyard gate, and looked about us. How long we remained there I cannot say, but the wind ceased just as suddenly as it had commenced. I glanced at my friend and saw that he was as white as a sheet, and he afterwards told me that I myself looked exactly the same.

"On we went without a word. Ten yards more brought us opposite the public-house, which was then owned by a Mrs. B., whose husband had died six months previously after a short illness, and was buried in the graveyard on our right. This house had two doors, one opening on the street through which we were passing, while the other was in a side street which led off this one. We were going by the house when suddenly we heard a terribly heavy knocking at the side door. I stopped immediately, and looked up that street, but nothing could be seen. We were just moving on again when from the side street there came terrible crying, as if a dog were in awful agony or were being severely punished. We went on and filled our can at the pump, and then returned to the engine-shed without any further incident.

"When I came off duty I returned home and went to bed. About mid-day I was awakened by some of the family who told me that Mrs. B. (the owner of the public-house) had had a stroke early that morning, and had died a couple of hours later."

VII

BANSHEES, AND OTHER DEATH-WARNINGS

O
F all Irish ghosts, fairies, or bogles, the Banshee (sometimes called locally the "Boheentha" or "Bankeentha") is the best known to the general public: indeed, cross-Channel visitors would class her with pigs, potatoes, and other fauna and flora of Ireland, and would expect her to make manifest her presence to them as being one of the sights of the country. She is a spirit with a lengthy pedigree—how lengthy no man can say, as its roots go back into the dim, mysterious past. The most famous Banshee of ancient times was that attached to the kingly house of O'Brien, Aibhill, who haunted the rock of Craglea above Killaloe, near the old palace of Kincora. In A.D. 1014 was fought the battle of Clontarf, from which the aged king, Brian Boru, knew that he would never come away alive, for the previous night Aibhill had appeared to him to tell him of his impending fate. The Banshee's method of foretelling death in olden times differed from that adopted by her at the present day: now she wails and wrings her hands, as a general rule, but in the old Irish tales she is to be found washing human heads and limbs, or blood-stained clothes, till the water is all dyed with human

blood—this would take place before a battle. So it would seem that in the course of centuries her attributes and characteristics have changed somewhat.

Very different descriptions are given of her personal appearance. Sometimes she is young and beautiful, sometimes old and of a fearsome appearance. One writer describes her as "a tall, thin woman with uncovered head, and long hair that floated round her shoulders, attired in something which seemed either a loose white cloak, or a sheet thrown hastily around her, uttering piercing cries." Another person, a coachman, saw her one evening sitting on a stile in the yard; she seemed to be a very small woman, with blue eyes, long light hair, and wearing a red cloak. Other descriptions will be found in this chapter. By the way, it does not seem to be true that the Banshee exclusively follows families of Irish descent, for the last incident had reference to the death of a member of a Co. Galway family English by name and origin.

One of the oldest and best-known Banshee stories is that related in the *Memoirs* of Lady Fanshawe.[11] In 1642 her husband, Sir Richard, and she chanced to visit a friend, the head of an Irish sept, who resided in his ancient baronial castle, surrounded with a moat. At midnight she was awakened by a ghastly and supernatural scream, and looking out of bed, beheld in the moonlight a female face and part of the form hovering at the window. The distance from the ground, as well as the circumstance of the moat, excluded the possibility that what she beheld was of this world. The face was that of a young and rather handsome

---

[11] Scott's *Lady of the Lake*, notes to Canto III (edition of 1811). A much better version of the story is to be found in H.C. Fanshawe, *Memoirs of Anne, Lady Fanshawe* (p. 57).

woman, but pale, and the hair, which was reddish, was loose and dishevelled. The dress, which Lady Fanshaw's terror did not prevent her remarking accurately, was that of the ancient Irish. This apparition continued to exhibit itself for some time, and then vanished with two shrieks similar to that which had first excited Lady Fanshaw's attention. In the morning, with infinite terror, she communicated to her host what she had witnessed, and found him prepared not only to credit, but to account for the superstition. "A near relation of my family," said he, "expired last night in this castle. We disguised our certain expectation of the event from you, lest it should throw a cloud over the cheerful reception which was your due. Now, before such an event happens in this family or castle, the female spectre whom you have seen is always visible. She is believed to be the spirit of a woman of inferior rank, whom one of my ancestors degraded himself by marrying, and whom afterwards, to expiate the dishonour done to his family, he caused to be drowned in the moat." In strictness this woman could hardly be termed a Banshee. The motive for the haunting is akin to that in the tale of the Scotch "Drummer of Cortachy," where the spirit of the murdered man haunts the family out of revenge, and appears before a death.

The late Mr. T. J. Westropp, M.A., furnished the following story: "My maternal grandmother heard the following tradition from her mother, one of the Miss Ross-Lewins, who witnessed the occurrence. Their father, Mr. Harrison Ross-Lewin, was away in Dublin on law business, and in his absence the young people went off to spend the evening with a friend who lived some miles away. The night was fine and lightsome as they were returning, save at one point where the road ran between trees or high hedges not far to the west of the old church of Kilchrist. The latter, like many similar ruins, was a simple oblong building, with long side-walls and high gables, and at that time it and its graveyard were unenclosed, and lay in the open fields. As the party passed down the long dark lane they suddenly heard in the distance loud keening and clapping of hands, as the country-people were accustomed to do when lamenting the dead. The Ross-Lewins hurried on, and came in sight of the church, on the side wall of which a little grey-haired old woman, clad in a dark cloak, was running to and fro, chanting and wailing, and throwing up her arms. The girls were very frightened, but the young men ran forward and surrounded the ruin, and two of them went into the church, the apparition vanishing from the wall as they did so. They searched every nook, and found no one, nor did anyone pass out. All were now well scared, and got home as fast as possible. On reaching their home their mother opened the door, and at once told them that she was in terror about their father, for, as she sat looking out the window in the moonlight, a huge raven with fiery eyes lit on the sill, and tapped three times on the glass. They told her their story, which only added to their anxiety, and as they stood talking, taps came to the nearest window, and they saw the bird again. A few days later news reached them that Mr. Ross-Lewin had died suddenly in Dublin. This occurred about 1776."

Mr. Westropp also writes that the sister of a former Roman Catholic Bishop told his sisters that when she was a little girl she went out one evening with some other children for a walk. Going down the road, they passed the gate of the principal demesne near the town. There was a rock, or large stone, beside the road, on which they saw something. Going nearer, they perceived it to be a little dark, old woman, who began crying and clapping her hands. Some of them attempted to speak to her, but got frightened, and all finally ran home as quickly as they could. Next day the news came that the gentleman, near whose gate the Banshee had cried, was dead, and it was found on inquiry that he had died at the very hour at which the children had seen the spectre.

A lady who is a relation of one of the compilers, and a member of a Co. Cork family of English descent, sends the two following experiences of a Banshee in her family. "My mother, when a young girl, was standing looking out of the window in their house at Blackrock, near Cork. She suddenly saw a white figure standing on a bridge which was easily visible from the house. The figure waved her arms towards the house, and my mother heard the bitter wailing of the Banshee. It lasted some seconds, and then the figure disappeared. Next morning my grandfather was walking as usual into the city of Cork. He accidentally fell, hit his head against the curb-stone, and never recovered consciousness.

"In March 1900, my mother was very ill, and one evening the nurse and I were with her arranging her bed. We suddenly heard the most extraordinary wailing, which seemed to come in waves round and under her bed. We naturally looked everywhere to try and find the cause, but in vain. The nurse and I looked at one another, but made no remark, as my mother did not seem to hear it. My sister was downstairs sitting with my father. She heard it, and thought some terrible thing had happened to her little boy, who was in bed upstairs. She rushed up, and found him sleeping quietly. My father did not hear it. In the house next door they heard it, and ran downstairs, thinking something had happened to the servant; but the latter at once said to them, 'Did you hear the Banshee? Mrs. P— must be dying.'"

A few years ago (*i.e.* before 1894) a curious incident occurred in a public school in connection with the belief in the Banshee. One of the boys, happening to become ill, was at once placed in a room by himself, where he used to sit all day. On one occasion, as he was being visited by the doctor, he suddenly started up from his seat, and affirmed that he heard somebody crying. The doctor, of course, who could hear or see nothing, came to the conclusion that the illness had slightly affected his brain. However, the boy, who appeared quite sensible, still persisted that he heard someone crying, and furthermore said, "It is the Banshee, as I have heard it before." The following morning the head-master received a telegram saying that the boy's brother had been accidentally shot dead.[12]

That the Banshee is not confined within the geographical limits of Ireland, but that she can follow the fortunes of a family abroad, and there foretell their death, is clearly shown by the following story. A party of visitors were gathered together on the deck of a private yacht on one of the Italian lakes, and during a lull in the conversation one of them, a Colonel, said to the owner, "Count, who's that queer-looking woman you have on board?" The Count replied that there was nobody except the ladies present, and the stewardess, but the speaker protested that he was correct, and suddenly, with a scream of horror, he placed his hands before his eyes, and exclaimed, "Oh, my God, what a face!" For some time he was overcome with terror, and at length reluctantly looked up, and cried:

"Thank Heavens, it's gone!"

"What was it?" asked the Count.

"Nothing human," replied the Colonel— "nothing belonging to this world. It was a woman of no earthly type, with a queer-

---

[12] A. G. Bradley, *Notes on some Irish Superstitions*, p. 9.

shaped, gleaming face, a mass of red hair, and eyes that would have been beautiful but for their expression, which was hellish. She had on a green hood, after the fashion of an Irish peasant."

An American lady present suggested that the description tallied with that of the Banshee, upon which the Count said:

"I am an O'Neill—at least I am descended from one. My family name is, as you know, Neilsini, which, little more than a century ago, was O'Neill. My great-grandfather served in the Irish Brigade, and on its dissolution at the time of the French Revolution had the good fortune to escape the general massacre of officers, and in company with an O'Brien and a Maguire fled across the frontier and settled in Italy. On his death his son, who had been born in Italy, and was far more Italian than Irish, changed his name to Neilsini, by which name the family has been known ever since. But for all that we are Irish."

"The Banshee was yours, then!" ejaculated the Colonel. "What exactly does it mean?"

"It means," the Count replied solemnly, "the death of someone very nearly associated with me. Pray Heaven it is not my wife or daughter."

On that score, however, his anxiety was speedily removed, for within two hours he was seized with a violent attack of angina pectoris, and died before morning.[13]

Mr. Elliott O'Donnell, to whose article on "Banshees" we are indebted for the above, adds: "The Banshee never manifests itself to the person whose death it is prognosticating. Other people may see or hear it, but the fated one never, so that when everyone

---

[13] *Occult Review* for September 1913.

present is aware of it but one, the fate of that one may be regarded as pretty well certain."

We must now pass on from the subject of Banshees to the kindred one of "Headless Coaches," the belief in which is widespread through the country. Apparently these dread vehicles must be distinguished from the phantom coaches, of which numerous circumstantial tales are also told. The first are harbingers of death, and in this connection are very often attached to certain families; the latter appear to be spectral phenomena pure and simple, whose appearance does not necessarily portend evil or death.

"At a house in Co. Limerick," writes Mr. T. J. Westropp, "occurred the remarkably-attested apparition of the headless coach in June 1806, when Mr. Ralph Westropp, my great-grandfather, lay dying. The story was told by his sons, John, William, and Ralph, to their respective children, who told it to me. They had sent for the doctor, and were awaiting his arrival in the dusk. As they sat on the steps they suddenly heard a heavy rumbling, and saw a huge dark coach drive into the paved court before the door. One of them went down to meet the doctor, but the coach swept past him, and drove down the avenue, which went straight between the fences and hedges to a gate. Two of the young men ran after the coach, which they could hear rumbling before them, and suddenly came full tilt against the avenue gate. The noise had stopped, and they were surprised at not finding the carriage. The gate proved to be locked, and when they at last awoke the lodge-keeper, he showed them the keys under his pillow; the doctor arrived a little later, but could do nothing, and the sick man died a few hours afterwards."

Two other good stories come from Co. Clare. One night in April 1821, two servants were sitting up to receive a son of the family,

Cornelius O'Callaghan, who had travelled in vain for his health, and was returning home. One of them, Halloran, said that the heavy rumble of a coach roused them. The other servant, Burke, stood on the top of the long flight of steps with a lamp, and sent Halloran down to open the carriage door. He reached out his hand to do so, saw a skeleton looking out, gave one yell, and fell in a heap. When the badly-scared Burke picked himself up there was no sign or sound of any coach. A little later the invalid arrived, so exhausted that he died suddenly in the early morning.

On the night of December 11, 1876, a servant of the MacNamaras was going his rounds at Ennistymon, a beautiful spot in a wooded glen, with a broad stream falling in a series of cascades. In the dark he heard the rumbling of wheels on the back avenue, and, knowing from the hour and place that no mortal vehicle could be coming, concluded that it was the death coach, and ran on, opening the gates before it. He had just time to open the third gate, and throw himself on his face beside it, when he heard a coach go clanking past. On the following day Admiral Sir Burton Macnamara died in London.

Mr. Westropp informs us that at sight or sound of this coach all gates should be thrown open, and then it will not stop at the house to call for a member of the family, but will only foretell the death of some relative at a distance. We hope our readers will carefully bear in mind this simple method of averting fate.

We may conclude this chapter with some account of strange and varied death-warnings, which are attached to certain families and foretell the coming of the King of Terrors.

In a Co. Wicklow family a death is preceded by the appearance of a spectre; the doors of the sitting-room open and a lady dressed in white satin walks across the room and hall. Before any member of a certain Queen's Co. family died a looking-glass was broken;

while in a branch of that family the portent was the opening and shutting of the avenue gate. In another Queen's Co. family approaching death was heralded by the cry of the cuckoo, no matter at what season of the year it might occur. A Mrs. F— and her son lived near Clonaslee. One day, in mid-winter, their servant heard a cuckoo; they went out for a drive, the trap jolted over a stone, throwing Mrs. F— and breaking her neck. The ringing of all the house-bells is another portent which seems to be attached to several families. In another the aeolian harp is heard at or before death; an account of this was given to the present writer by a clergyman, who declares that he heard it in the middle of the night when one of his relatives passed away. A death-warning in the shape of a white owl follows the Westropp family. This last appeared, it is said, before a death in 1909, but, as Mr. T. J. Westropp remarks, it would be more convincing if it appeared at places where the white owl does *not* nest and fly out every night. No doubt this list might be drawn out to much greater length.

In front of the residence of the G. family in Co. Galway there is, or formerly was, a round ring of grass surrounded by a low evergreen hedge. The lady who related this story to our informant stated that one evening dinner was kept waiting for Mr. G., who was absent in town on some business. She went out on the hall-door steps in order to see if the familiar trot of the carriage horses could be heard coming down the road. It was a bright moonlight night, and as she stood there she heard a child crying with a peculiar whining cry, and distinctly saw a small childlike figure running round and round the grass ring inside the evergreen hedge, and casting a shadow in the moonlight. Going into the house she casually mentioned this as a peculiar circumstance to Mrs. G., upon which, to her surprise, that lady nearly fainted, and got into a terrible state of nervousness. Recovering a little, she told her that this crying and figure were always heard and seen whenever any member met with an accident or before a death. A messenger was immediately sent to meet Mr. G., who was found lying senseless on the road, as the horses had taken fright and bolted, flinging him out and breaking the carriage-pole.

A woman in white follows the family of Coplen Langford, of Kilcosgriff Castle, Co. Limerick, and manifests herself when any member is about to die. The traditional account of her origin, as well as of some of the occasions on which she appeared, have a been furnished to present a writer by Mr. Richard Coplen Langford, J. P., of Kilcosgriff.

Over two hundred years ago William Langford, a young man who was in the Army, returned suddenly on leave to Kilcosgriff, and finding that the house was full of guests declared that he would sleep in what was then known as the Haunted Chamber. When retiring for the night he placed a pair of pistols on a small table beside his bed, thinking that someone might try to play a practical joke on him, in which event he would give the intruders a good fright. About midnight, when he was going to sleep, he saw the door open slowly, and a lady clad in her night attire, and carrying a lighted candle, enter the room. He pretended to be asleep, but watched her through his half-closed eyelids, and perceived that she had a magnificent diamond ring on her hand. She came slowly to his bedside, bent over and looked at him, then turning down the clothes, got into bed beside him and extinguished the light. He gently put his hand out and touched the hand on which sparkled the ring. He found it, as he had expected, warm flesh and blood; the lady was one of the guests, and was given to walking in her sleep. So he took the ring off her finger, and put it on one of his own. After a very short time she got up, relit the candle, and walked out of the room.

Next morning Mr. Langford came down to the breakfast-room, where all the guests were assembled. While eating his breakfast he displayed the ring somewhat ostentatiously; on catching sight of it sparkling on his finger a young lady, who was a stranger to him, was seized with faintness and had to leave the table. After breakfast, as Mr. Langford was sitting on a seat outside the hall door, the same lady came to him and said:

"Will you tell me where you got that ring? I recognise it as mine, but surely you did not dare to come into my room and take it!"

"Most certainly I did not," he replied. "But to tell you the exact truth *you* came into *my* room and into my bed, and it was then that I took it off your pretty hand. Take it back," he added. "And when you are doing so you may as well take me with it!" Blushingly she said yes to his unusual method of proposal, and so they were married and lived happily. She was Miss Gertrude St. Ledger, sister to the first Viscount Doneraile, and married William Langford in 1703. When she was dying she told her husband that she would be seen when a death was about to take place in the family.

Such is the tradition, briefly told, of the origin of the White Lady. Our correspondent, Mr. Richard Langford, sends the account of four of her appearances, three of which he witnessed himself.

"My father told me that one night a black setter dog of his got up on one of the piers of the yard-gate and commenced to howl most dismally. He went out to it in his nightgown, but could not get it to come down. Suddenly he saw a woman walk across the yard; he called out to her, but she returned no answer, and walked on till she went through a door into a stable. He followed her, but found nothing there except the horse. He returned to bed, but the dog continued howling all night, and in the morning he learnt of the death of his father at Miltown Malbay. This occurred in September 1856.

"When the latter's wife, my grandmother, died, I was in the dining-room here, and had a most unearthly crying in the deer-park. I called to my brother, who was in the nursery (as we termed a certain room) to come and listen; as soon as he came it stopped, so he went away laughing at me. It soon commenced again, and on looking out of the window I saw a white figure move along a path by the garden, which I called the Lovers' Walk. It was then getting fairly dark. I was startled somewhat, but called out, whereupon the figure disappeared in a clump of laurels. I went out after it, and carefully examined the spot, but could find no trace of anyone. That night my grandmother died.

"In 1889, during my father's last illness I was sitting in the dining-room with no society save that of the family portraits. My father's room was at the end of a long passage; he would have no nurse, and we all had to look after him. I heard movement outside the dining-room door, so I went and looked out. I was about to walk to see how my father was, when suddenly the white figure of a woman glided by me. I followed her but she vanished, so I hastened to my father's room, only to find that he had just breathed his last.

"My youngest brother, Crawford Langford of Glenville, had been in failing health for some time, and had gone to Dublin to consult doctors. On his return he was invited by my cousin, Major Langford, D.S.O., of The Abbey, Rathkeale, to go and stay there with him for a few days' change. While there he got worse, and the doctor said it would not be safe to move him. He had two nurses in attendance. On the evening of February 1, 1914, I with one of the nurses was sitting in his room at the Abbey at five o'clock. Tea was announced, so I said to the nurse, 'You go down and have tea, and I shall remain here.' I was seated with my back towards the fireplace on a lounge opposite to the sick man's bed. Suddenly the door opened, and a tall figure of a lady in white walked or rather glided into the room. She went over to my brother's bed, put her arm across him, smiled at him, then looked at me and smiled, and then vanished. I wished to speak to her, but my powers of utterance failed me. My brother died six days later."

A lady correspondent states that her cousin, a Sir Patrick Dun's nurse, was attending a case in the town of Wicklow. Her patient was a middle-aged woman, the wife of a well-to-do shopkeeper. One evening the nurse was at her tea in the dining-room beneath the sick-room, when suddenly she heard a tremendous crash overhead. Fearing her patient had fallen out of bed, she hurried upstairs, to find her dozing quietly, and there was not the least sign of any disturbance. A member of the family, to whom she related this, told her calmly that that noise was always heard in their house before the death of any of them, and that it was a sure sign that the invalid would not recover. Contrary to the nurse's expectations, she died the following day.

Knocking on the door is another species of death-warning. The Rev. D. B. Knox writes: "On the evening before the wife of a clerical friend of mine died, the knocker of the hall-door was loudly rapped. All in the room heard it. The door was opened, but there was no one there. Again the knocker was heard, but no one was to be seen when the door was again opened. A young man, brother of the dying woman, went into the drawing-room, and looked through one of the drawing-room windows. The full light of the moon fell on the door, and as he looked the knocker was again lifted and loudly rapped."

Another somewhat similar story was related by a lady who is

BANSHEES, AND OTHER DEATH-WARNINGS

well known to the present a writer, but who, for family reasons, does not wish to have her name published.

"Some years ago my husband and I lived in a residential suburb in Dublin. As our house was a large one we shared it with my husband's father and mother. One winter—I cannot remember if it was before or after Christmas—my mother-in-law was ill, though she did not die until the following summer. My husband and I were sitting by the dining-room fire in the evening, when there came a loud knocking at the hall door. As the maid was out for the evening, I went and opened the door myself, but found no one outside. As this was a quiet residential district, and as the houses were separated from the road by gardens, I knew that it could not be mischievous children giving a 'run away knock.' Somewhat mystified I returned to the dining-room, and told my husband. He at once replied, 'That is the knocking that follows the family whenever a death is about to occur!'

"My mother-in-law died the following July. In the interval between her death and burial, I heard a knocking at the door. I went to open it, thinking of course that some friends or relations were coming in, but to my surprise I found no one on the doorstep; and, what was still more peculiar, the crape-covered locker was up, as if someone were about to complete a knock. I did not see it fall, however, while I was there, nor was there any further knocking. I told some of my people-in-law who were in the house at the time, and they too said that it was the knocking that followed the family."

The following portent occurs in a Co. Cork family. At one time the lady of the house lay ill, and her two daughters were aroused one night by screams proceeding from their mother's room. They rushed in, and found her sitting up in bed, staring at some object unseen to them, but which, from the motion of her eyes, appeared to be moving across the floor. When she became calm she told them, what they had not known before, that members of the family were sometimes warned of the death, or approaching death, of some other member by the appearance of a ball of fire, which would pass slowly through the room; this phenomenon she had just witnessed. A day or two afterwards the mother heard of the death of her brother, who lived in the Colonies.

A strange appearance, known as the "Scanlan Lights," is connected with the family of Scanlan of Ballyknockane, Co. Limerick, and is seen frequently at the death of a member. The traditional origin of the lights is connected with a well-known Irish legend, which we give here briefly. Scanlan Mor (died A.D. 640), King of Ossory, from whom the family claim descent, was suspected of disaffection by Aedh mac Ainmire, Ard-Righ of Ireland, who cast him into prison, and loaded him with fetters. When St. Columcille attended the Synod of Drom Ceat, he besought Aedh to free his captive, but the Ard-Righ churlishly refused; whereupon Columcille declared that he should be freed, and that that very night he should unloose his (the Saint's) brogues. Columcille went away, and that night a bright pillar of fire appeared in the air, and hung over the house where Scanlan was imprisoned. A beam of light darted into the room where he lay, and a voice called to him, bidding him rise, and shake off his fetters. In amazement he did so, and was led out past his guards by an angel. He made his way to Columcille, with whom he was to continue that night, and as the Saint stooped down to unloose his brogues Scanlan anticipated him, as he had prophesied.[14]

---

[14] Canon Carrigan, in his *History of the Diocese of Ossory* (I. 32 intro.), shows that this legend should rather be connected with Scanlan son of Ceannfaeladh.

Such appears to be the traditional origin of the "Scanlan lights." Our correspondent adds: "These are always seen at the demise of a member of the family. We have ascertained that by the present head of the family (Scanlan of Ballyknockane) they were seen, first, as a pillar of fire with radiated crown at the top; and secondly, inside the house, by the room being lighted up brightly in the night. By other members of the family now living these lights have been seen in the shape of balls of fire of various sizes." The above was copied from a private manuscript written some few years ago. Our correspondent further states: "I also have met with four persons in this county [Limerick] who have seen the lights on Knockfierna near Ballyknockane before the death of a Scanlan, one of the four being the late head of the family and owner, William Scanlan, J.P., who saw the flames on the hill-side on the day of his aunt's death some years ago. The last occasion was as late as 1913, on the eve of the death of a Scanlan related to the present owner of Ballyknockane."

But of all the death-warnings in connection with Irish families surely the strangest is the Gormanstown foxes. The crest of that noble family is a running fox, while the same animal also forms one of the supporters of the coat-of-arms. The story is, that when the head of the house is dying the foxes—not spectral foxes, but creatures of flesh and blood—leave the coverts and congregate at Gormanstown Castle.

Let us see what proof there is of this. When Jenico, the 12th Viscount, was dying in 1860, foxes were seen about the house and moving towards the house for some days previously. Just before his death three foxes were playing about and making a noise close to the house, and just in front of the "cloisters," which are yew-trees planted and trained in that shape. The Hon. Mrs. Farrell states as regards the same that the foxes came in pairs into the demesne, and sat under the Viscount's bedroom window, and barked and howled all night. Next morning they were to be found crouching about in the grass in front and around the house. They walked through the poultry and never touched them. After the funeral they disappeared.

At the death of Edward, the 13th Viscount, in 1876, the foxes were also there. He had been rather better one day, but the foxes appeared, barking under the window, and he died that night contrary to expectation.

On October 28, 1907, Jenico, the 14th Viscount, died in Dublin. About 8 o'clock that night the coachman and gardener saw two foxes near the chapel (close to the house), five or six more round the front of the house, and several crying in the "cloisters." Two days later the Hon. Richard Preston, R.F.A., was watching by his father's body in the above chapel. About 3 A.M. he became conscious of a slight noise, which seemed to be that of a number of people walking stealthily around the chapel on the gravel walk. He went to the side door, listened, and heard outside a continuous and insistent snuffling or sniffing noise, accompanied by whimperings and scratchings at the door. On opening it he saw a full-grown fox sitting on the path within four feet of him. Just in the shadow was another, while he could hear several more moving close by in the darkness. He then went to the end door, opposite the altar, and on opening it saw two more foxes, one so close that he could have touched it with his foot. On shutting the door the noise continued till 5 A.M., when it suddenly ceased.[15]

---

[15] *New Ireland Review* for April 1908, by permission of the publishers, Messrs Sealy, Bryers, & Walker.

VIII

MISCELLANEOUS SUPERNORMAL EXPERIENCES

THE matter in this chapter does not seem, strictly speaking, to come under the head of any of the preceding ones: it contains no account of houses or places permanently haunted, or of warnings of impending death. Rather we have gathered up in it a number of tales relative to the appearance of the "wraiths" of living men, or accounts of visions, strange apparitions, or extraordinary experiences; some few of these have a purpose, while the majority are strangely aimless and purposeless—something is seen or heard, that is all, and no results, good or bad, follow.

We commence with one which, however, certainly indicates a purpose which was fulfilled. It is the experience of Mrs. Seymour, wife to one of the compilers. When she was a little girl she resided in Dublin; amongst the members of the family was her paternal grandmother. This old lady was not as kind as she might have been to her grand-daughter, and consequently the latter was somewhat afraid of her. In process of time the grandmother died. Mrs. Seymour, who was then about eight years of age, had to pass the door of the room where the death occurred in order to reach her own bedroom, which was a flight higher up. Past this door the child used to fly in terror with all possible speed. On one occasion, however, as she was preparing to make the usual rush past, she distinctly felt a hand placed on her shoulder, and became conscious of a voice saying, "Don't be afraid, Mary!" From that day on the child never had the least feeling of fear, and always walked quietly past the door.

The Rev. D. B. Knox sends a curious personal experience, which was shared by him with three other people. He writes as follows: "Not very long ago my wife and I were preparing to retire for the night. A niece, who was in the house, was in her bedroom and the door was open. The maid had just gone to her room. All four of us distinctly heard the heavy step of a man walking along the corridor, apparently in the direction of the bathroom. We searched the whole house immediately, but no one was discovered. Nothing untoward happened except the death of the maid's mother about a fortnight later. It was a detached house, so that the noise could not have been made by the neighbours."

A Canon of the Church of Ireland has sent a curious experience, and one which was shared by his little daughter. He writes as follows:

"When I had been incumbent of A—, Co. Galway, for about three years, I was awakened one early morning by the singular conviction that someone had entered the room. I looked about me, and saw an elderly man, with a red muffler wrapped round his neck, carrying a lighted candle in his hand. Behind him was a more shadowy figure, as if someone was following him. I rubbed my eyes, and concluded that it was all a dream, when suddenly my little girl of three years of age, who was lying in a cot beside my bed, cried out loudly, 'Oh, Papa—the man! The man!' and to this day (she is now the mother of two children) she affirms that she saw the apparition. I had never seen my predecessor in the parish, but from the descriptions which have been given me of him he corresponded to the figure I beheld. He usually wore a red muffler, and towards the end of his life generally had a male attendant following him. Furthermore, the room I was then occupying had been his bedroom. But if his spirit visited me I am sure I have no idea for what purpose it came, as it made no attempt at communication."

In the following tale the "double" or "wraith" of a living man was seen by three different people, one of whom, our correspondent, saw it through a telescope. She writes: "In May 1883 the parish of A— was vacant, so Mr. D—, the Diocesan Curate, used to come out to take service on Sundays. One day there were two funerals to be taken, the one at a graveyard some distance off, the other at A— churchyard. My brother was at both, the far-off one being taken the first. The house we then lived in looked down towards A— churchyard, which was about a quarter of a mile away. From an upper window my sister and I saw two surpliced figures going out to meet the coffin, and said, 'Why, there are two clergy!' having supposed that there would be only Mr. D—. I, being short-sighted, used a telescope, and saw the two surplices showing between the people. But when my brother returned he said, 'A strange thing has happened. Mr. D— and Mr. W— (curate of a neighbouring parish) took the far-off funeral. I saw them both again at A— but when I went into the vestry I only saw Mr. W— I asked where Mr. D— was, and he replied that he had left immediately after the first funeral, as he had to go to Kilkenny, and that he (Mr. W—) had come on *alone* to take the funeral at A—.'"

Here is a curious account of what seems to have been a phantom funeral! A gentleman writes:

"One night in the month of March 1898 I was driving home with two companions from the house of a relative. We were talking about things in general as our horse trotted leisurely along the lonely midnight road. Things eerie were far from our thoughts. The night was fairly dark, and we had no lamps. When about half-way on our journey, we saw an object coming slowly towards us. Owing to the imperfect light, we did not notice it until it was within ten yards of our horse's head. It was travelling fair in the middle of the road, and our horse swerved slightly of his own accord before I could pull the rein, and the object also swerved a little to the opposite side. But for this, there would apparently have been a collision.

"No sooner had we passed than we three stared interrogatively at one another. After a moment or two, I exclaimed, 'What in Heaven's name is that? Or did you fellows see anything?'

"From their replies they had both seen it as distinctly as I had; and their descriptions tallied in the main with mine.

"After a good deal of discussion we agreed that the object we had met so unexpectedly was more like a coffin than anything else; and from its slow, swaying motion it appeared to be carried along by invisible bearers. Its height from the ground—some two or three feet—as it moved towards us and past us confirmed this view.

"We saw nothing whatever but the moving coffin—if it was a coffin; and we heard absolutely nothing. There were no bearers, and there was no procession of mourners.

"I may mention that in this country (Wexford) the coffins of the poor are frequently borne to the cemetery by the aid of sheets passed under the coffin and brough through the handles at the sides. Biers on which corpses are borne shoulder-high are not much used.

"I may add that none of us experienced any creepy or uncanny feeling on the occasion, and we were not in the least afraid, even after the passing of the 'ghost.' We were puzzled and curious and intensely interested—that was all."

Mr. Thomas Fahey, a young farmer well known to the present writer, had a very eerie experience on a stetch of the road due north of Donohil Rectory. He says:

"One autumn evening, about four years ago, I was cycling home from the village of Cappawhite, and going in the direction of Ironmills Bridge. Every inch of the road was well known to me, as I had travelled it hundreds of times. About a third of a mile from the bridge there is a cottage on the left-hand side of the road, the garden of which is bounded by a bohereen, which leads up into the fields. From this point the road, which has hitherto been on a gentle incline, dips down steeply for a hundred yards or so, until a second bohereen is reached, which also leads up to the left to some cottages; from this latter point, it runs down at a fair incline to the cross-roads at the bridge.

"It was after 10 o'clock, and the night was fairly dark, though there was sufficient light for me to see my way, and distinguish the objects around me, without the aid of a lamp. I was passing the cottage at the commencement of the hill, and was about to free-wheel, when suddenly something came out of the bohereen—I cannot tell how it progressed, whether it rolled over, walked or flew—and rested on the handle-bars of the bicycle. In appearance this thing resembled a large round bundle, and seemed black in colour; it cannot have been an animal, as it made neither sound nor movement, and emitted no odour. It lay on the handle-bars, and filled all the space between to such an extent that I had to sit bolt upright with my head well back to avoid touching it with my face; it did not come above the level of my eyes, and I did not feel it against my hand. Under the shock of this sudden impact the machine wobbled for a moment, but I soon righted it, and considered that the best thing for me to do under the circumstances was to keep on moving. I felt no impact when the thing came on the handle-bars, as one would have felt if an animal had sprung on them; but no sooner was it there than the bicycle became so heavy that I had actually to *pedal hard* to get down a hill where normally I used the free-wheel and braked.

"I pedalled down this hill until I reached to the second bohereen, when the thing disappeared as suddenly as it had come. Where or how it went, I cannot say. Relieved of this weight, the bicycle bounded on, and I free-wheeled down the remainder of the road until I reached the bridge. I cannot offer any explanation of this weird experience, and I never met anyone who could."

Here we give a strange tale from the city of Limerick of a lady's "double" being seen, with no consequent results. It is sent by Mr. Richard Hogan as the personal experience of his sister, Mrs. Mary Murnane. On Saturday, October 25, 1913, at half-past four o'clock in the afternoon, Mr. Hogan left the house in order to purchase some cigarettes. A quarter of an hour afterwards Mrs. Murnane went down the town to do some business. As she was walking down George Street she saw a group of four persons standing on the pavement engaged in conversation. They were: her brother, a Mr. O'S—, and two ladies, a Miss P. O'D—, and her sister, Miss M. O'D—. She recognised the latter, as her face was partly turned towards her, and noted that she was dressed in a knitted coat, and light blue hat, while in her left hand she held a bag or purse; the other lady's back was turned towards her. As Mrs. Murnane was in a hurry to get her business done she determined to pass them by without being noticed, but a number of people coming in the opposite direction blocked the way, and compelled her to walk quite close to the group of four; but they were so intent on listening to what one lady was saying that they took no notice of her. The speaker appeared to be Miss M. O'D—, and, though Mrs. Murnane did not actually hear her *speak* as she passed her, yet from their attitudes the other three seemed to be listening to what she was saying, and she heard her laugh when right behind her not the laugh of her sister P.— and the *laugh* was repeated after she had left the group a little behind.

So far there is nothing out of the common. When Mrs. Murnane returned to her house about an hour later she found her brother Richard there before her. She casually mentioned to him how she had passed him and his three companions on the pavement. To which he replied that she was quite correct except in one point, namely that there were only *three* in the group, as M. O'D— *was not present* as she had not come to Limerick at all that day. She then described to him the exact position each one of the four occupied, and the clothes worn by them; to all of which facts he assented, except as to the presence of Miss M. O'D—. Mrs. Murnane adds, "That is all I can say in the matter, but most certainly the fourth person was in the group, as I both saw and heard her. She wore the same clothes I had seen on her previously, with the exception of the hat; but the following Saturday she had on the same coloured hat I had seen on her the previous Saturday. When I told her about it she was as much mystified as I was and am. My brother stated that there was no laugh from any of the three present."

Mrs. G. Kelly sends an experience of a "wraith," which seems in some mysterious way to have been conjured up in her mind by the description she had heard, and then externalised. She writes: "About four years ago a musical friend of ours was staying in the house. He and my husband were playing and singing Dvorak's *Spectre's Bride,* a work which he had studied with the composer himself. This music appealed very much to both, and they were excited and enthusiastic over it. Our friend was giving many personal reminiscences of Dvorak, and his method of explaining the way he wanted his work done. I was sitting by, an interested listener, for some time. On getting up at last, and going into the drawing-room, I was startled and somewhat frightened to find a man standing there in a shadowy part of the room. I saw him distinctly, and could describe his appearance accurately. I called out, and the two men ran in, but as the apparition only lasted for a second, they were too late. I described the man whom I had seen, whereupon our friend exclaimed, 'Why, that was Dvorak himself!' At that time I had never seen a picture of Dvorak, but when our friend returned to London he sent me one which I recognised as the likeness of the man whom I had seen in our drawing-room."

A curious vision, a case of second sight, in which a quite unimportant event, previously unknown, was revealed, is sent by the percipient, who is a lady well known to both the compilers, and a life-long friend of one of them. She says: "Last summer I sent a cow to the fair of Limerick, a distance of about thirteen miles, and the men who took her there the day before the fair left her in a paddock for the night close to Limerick city. I awoke up very early next morning, and was fully awake when I saw (not with my ordinary eyesight, but apparently inside my head) a light, an intensely brilliant light, and in it I saw the back gate being opened by a red-haired woman and the cow I had supposed in the fair walking through the gate. I then knew that the cow must be home, and going to the yard later on I was met by the wife of the man who was in charge in a great state of excitement.

'Oh law! Miss,' she exclaimed, 'you'll be mad! Didn't Julia [a red-haired woman] find the cow outside the lodge gate as she was going out at 4 o'clock to the milking!' That's my tale—perfectly true, and I would give a good deal to be able to control that light, and see more if I could."

Another curious vision was seen by a lady who is also a friend of both the compilers. One night she was kneeling at her bedside saying her prayers (hers was the only bed in the room), when suddenly she felt a distinct touch on her shoulder. She turned round in the direction of the touch and saw at the end of the room a bed, with a pale, indistinguishable figure laid therein, and what appeared to be a clergyman standing over it. About a week later she fell into a long and dangerous illness in which she was attended by a clergyman—the present writer.

An account of a dream which implied an extraordinary coincidence, if coincidence it be and nothing more, was sent as follows by a correspondent, who requested that no names be published. "That which I am about to relate has a peculiar interest for me, inasmuch as the central figure in it was my own grand-aunt, and moreover the principal witness (if I may use such a term) was my father. At the period during which this strange incident occurred my father was living with his aunt and some other relatives.

"One morning at the breakfast-table, my grand-aunt announced that she had had a most peculiar dream during the previous night. My father, who was always very interested in that kind of thing, took down in his notebook all the particulars concerning it. They were as follows.

"My grand-aunt dreamt that she was in a cemetery, which she recognised as Glasnevin, and as she gazed at the memorials of the dead which lay so thick around, one stood out most conspicuously, and caught her eye, for she saw clearly cut on the cold white stone *an inscription bearing her own name:*

CLARE. S. D—
Died 14th of March, 1873
Dearly loved and ever mourned.
R.I.P.

while, to add to the peculiarity of it, the date on the stone as given above was, from the day of her dream, exactly a year in advance.

"My grand-aunt was not very nervous, and soon the dream faded from her mind. Months rolled by, and one morning at breakfast it was noticed that my grand-aunt had not appeared, but as she was a very religious woman it was thought that she had gone out to church. However, as she did not appear my father sent someone to her room to see if she were there, and as no answer was given to repeated knocking the door was opened, and my grand-aunt was found kneeling at her bedside, dead. The day of her death was March 14, 1873, corresponding exactly with the date seen in her dream a twelvemonth before. My grand-aunt was buried in Glasnevin, and on her tombstone (a white marble slab) was placed the inscription which she had read in her dream." Our correspondent sent us a photograph of the stone and its inscription.

An even more extraordinary dream—if one is satisfied with describing it as a dream—was experienced in his youth by Mr. Thomas S. Hill, of Donnybrook, Co. Dublin. He tells his story as follows:

"Thirty years ago, when I was ten years old and acted as an altar-boy in the parochial church of one of the principal towns in Co. Kildare, a young priest, a particular favourite of mine, died. The remains were brought to the church, where (as is usual) they lay, dressed in Mass vestments, in an open coffin in front of the high altar. As well as I can remember, some relatives of the deceased cleric arrived from across the Channel for the obsequies; at all events, owing to the want of a suitable train, they were obliged to travel on a side-car from the distant port of Rosslare, and I did not arrive at the town till about 11.45 P.M.

"In the meantime, the clerk of the church (who still occupies that position, and to whom *I* told my story that night) and I had closed up the church at 9.30 P.M., Requiem Vespers being over at 8.30. Priests and people had withdrawn and 10.15 found the clerk and myself alone with the dead, and awaiting the arrival of the relatives. At 10.30 the clerk's sister called to say that her mother, who had been an invalid for years, was almost breathing her last. I insisted on the clerk accompanying his sister to the bedside of his mother, who died within the hour. Thus I was left to myself alone with the dead in that huge church, the only light being that which came from the six mourning candles around the catafalque and the sanctuary lamp. I confess, I felt some uneasiness; the side-aisles, confessionals, and statues could be but dimly perceived in the faint light, and the empty fane seemed full of mysterious possibilities—can I be blamed at such an age for wishing myself safe at home in bed! I rose in my fear, beside my dead friend, looked at him, and recited aloud a fervent *De Profundis* for the repose of his soul. I then took from a book-case an illustrated Bible History such as the elder boys were accustomed to use at Sunday's catechism classes. Then I resumed my seat beside the coffin and commenced to read in order to occupy my thoughts.

"The next thing I remember is that I found myself nodding; the sacristy clock struck an hour (probably eleven), and the book fell from my hand and made a noise on the ground. At this moment the dead priest descended or rather floated from the coffin; he looked at me, and called me by name, saying, 'Thomas, come!' I followed him inside the communion rails, he ascended the altar steps, and I repaired to the sacristy to prepare to serve Mass. I hurriedly vested myself in surplice and soutane, brought out the Missal, and the cruets filled with wine and water, and lighted the two usual week-morning Mass-candles. I was conscious of nothing supernatural during these operations, and felt neither fear nor excitement; the dominant thought in my mind was that I was about to serve Mass, was pressed for time, and that the priest was waiting for me. I served Mass quite normally. I never gave myself the habit of looking about me on such occasions, and I did not do so now; but I 'sensed' the presence of a very large congregation!

"After Mass I preceded the priest to the sacristy; we both bowed to the great crucifix there, then to each other, and I left him unvesting at the usual bench. I brought in the cruets and Missal, and extinguished the altar candles. When I left the Missal in the vestment-press I found the priest had taken his departure. I then replaced the extinguisher on its hook in a long narrow press, and—awoke! While I was still rubbing my eyes I was joined by the clerk, to whom I related my extraordinary story. On hearing it he set out to investigate, and I accompanied him. Nothing seemed to be disturbed in the sacristy; the cruets, lavabo basin, and towel were quite dry, and ready for the morning Mass. The Bible History was at my feet, but—*I was attired in surplice and soutane!*

"For the benefit of those who are unacquainted with our ceremonial I should add that I had been so attired for Requiem Vespers, but as soon as that service was over I had discarded these as usual with the other servers (I had swung the censer at vespers). It would have been most irregular to have done anything else, or to have continued wearing these vestments after the conclusion of service; had I inadvertently done so the clerk would have noticed it, and would have drawn my attention to the fact."

The late Archdeacon of Limerick, Ven. J. A. Haydn, LL.D., sent the following experience: "In the year 1870 I was rector of the little rural parish of Chapel Russell. One autumn day the rain fell with a quiet, steady, and hopeless persistence from morning to night. Wearied at length from the gloom, and tired of reading and writing, I determined to walk to the church about half a mile away, and pass a half-hour playing the harmonium, returning for the lamp-light and tea.

"I wrapped up, put the key of the church in my pocket, and started. Arriving at the church, I walked up the straight avenue, bordered with graves and tombs on either side, while the soft, steady rain quietly pattered on the trees. When I reached the church door, before putting the key in the lock, moved by some indefinable impulse, I stood on the doorstep, turned round, and looked back upon the path I had just trodden. My amazement may be imagined when I saw, seated on a low, tabular tombstone close to the avenue, a lady with her back towards me. She was wearing a black velvet jacket or short cape, with a narrow border of vivid white: her head, and luxuriant jet-black hair, were surmounted by a hat of the shape and make that I think used to be called at that time a 'turban'; it was also of black velvet, with a snow-white wing or feather at the right-hand side of it. It may be seen how deliberately and minutely I observed the appearance, when I can thus recall it after more than forty years.

"Actuated by a desire to attract the attention of the lady, and induce her to look towards me, I noisily inserted the key in the door, and suddenly opened it with a rusty crack. Turning round to see the effect of my policy—the lady was gone!—vanished! Not yet daunted, I hurried to the place, which was not ten paces away, and closely searched the stone and the space all round it, but utterly in vain; there were absolutely no traces of the late presence of a human being! I may add that nothing particular or remarkable followed the singular apparition, and that I never heard anything calculated to throw any light on the mystery."

A lady send the account of the experience of herself, and of her brother son another occasion, in an old house in the neighbourhood of Tinahely, Co. Wicklow, which seems to have its fitting place in this chapter, as it hardly comes under the head of Haunted Houses.

"One summer night, when I was in my fifteenth the year, I was awakened by a noise occurring at the servants' door, which was on the opposite side of the lobby, about eighteen feet away. I got up and looked out, and saw a very tall draped white figure, about seven feet high. I was terrified, and felt a cold perspiration break out all over me. I rushed back into bed, and pulled all the bed-clothes over my head. While lying so covered, I heard the clock in the hall strike one. Then I started for my mother's room with all the bed-clothes still over my head, sobbing hysterically. All that summer I slept wretchedly until I went away for a change of air.

"Many years later I was out driving with my brother, when something made me tell this story, and as I mentioned the hour my brother gave an exclamation of astonishment, and said, 'Exactly the same happened to me at that hour one night, when I was about seventeen, except that the ghost came right into my room, and stood plucking at the bed-clothes.' He added that he rushed past it into my parents' room, and stayed there for the rest of the night. Neither he nor I saw any apparition either before or since.

Here is a story of a ghost who knew what it wanted—and got it! "In the part of Co. Wicklow from which my people come," writes a Miss D—, "there was a family who were not exactly related, but of course of the clan. Many years ago a young daughter, aged about twenty, died. Before her death she had directed her parents to bury her in a certain graveyard. But for some reason they did not do so, and from that hour she gave them no peace. She appeared to them at all hours, especially when they went to the well for water. So distracted were they, that at length they got permission to exhume the remains and have them reinterred in the desired graveyard. This they did by torchlight—a weird scene truly! I can vouch for the truth of this latter portion, at all events, as some of my own relatives were present."

Mr. T. J. Westropp contributes a tale of a ghost of an unusual type, *i.e.* one which actually did communicate matters of importance to his family. "A lady who related many ghost stories to me, also told me how, after her father's death, the family could not find some papers or receipts of value. One night she awoke, and heard a sound which she at once recognised as the footsteps of her father, who was lame. The door creaked, and she prayed that she might be able to see him. Her prayer was granted: she saw him distinctly holding a yellow parchment book tied with tape. 'F—, child,' said he, 'this is the book your mother is looking for. It is in the third drawer of the cabinet near the cross-door; tell your mother to be more careful in future about business papers.' Incontinent he vanished, and she at once awoke her mother, in whose room she was sleeping, who was very angry and ridiculed the story, but the girl's earnestness at length impressed her. She got up, went to the old cabinet, and at once found the missing book in the third drawer."

Here is another tale of an equally useful and obliging ghost.

"A gentleman, a relative of my own," writes a lady, "often received warnings from his dead father of things that were about to happen. Besides the farm on which he lived, he had another some miles away which adjoined a large demesne. Once in a great storm a fir-tree was blown down in the demesne, and fell into his field. The woodranger came to him and told him he might as well cut up the tree, and take it away. Accordingly one day he set out for this purpose, taking with him two men and a cart. He got into the fields by a stile, while his men went on to a gate. As he appoached a gap between two fields he saw, standing in it, his father as plainly as he ever saw him in life, and beckoning him back warningly. Unable to understand this, he still advanced, whereupon his father looked very angry, and his gestures became imperious. This induced him to turn away, so he sent his men home, and left the tree uncut. He subsequently discovered that a plot had been laid by the woodranger, who coveted his farm, and who hoped to have him dispossessed by accusing him of stealing the tree."

A clergyman in the diocese of Clogher gave a personal experience of table-turning to the present Dean of St. Patrick's,[16] who kindly sent the same to the writer. He said: "When I was a young man, I met some friends one evening, and we decided to amuse ourselves with table-turning. The local dispensary was vacant at the time, so we said that if the table would work we should ask who would be appointed as medical officer. As we sat round it touching it with our hands it began to knock. We said:

"'Who are you?'

---

[16] The late Very Rev. C. T. Ovenden, D. D.

"The table spelt out the name of a Bishop of the Church of Ireland. We asked, thinking that the answer was absurd, as we knew him to be alive and well:

"'Are you dead?'

"The table answered, 'Yes.'

"We laughed at this and asked:

"'Who will be appointed to the dispensary?'

"The table spelt out the name of a stranger, who was not one of the candidates, whereupon we left off, thinking that the whole thing was nonsense.

"The next morning I saw in the papers that the Bishop in question had died that afternoon about two hours before our meeting, and a few days afterwards I saw the name of the stranger as the new dispensary doctor. I got such a shock that I determined never to have anything to do with table-turning again."

A very extraordinary account of weird and unpleasant happenings, apparently because automatic writing was practised, is sent by a lady whose lot it was to experience these, and who desires to remain anonymous.

"The events which I am about to record took place in a quiet country house in a lovely part of Ireland. Beyond the fact that they occurred between 1908 and 1911 I cannot give the date—as far as I remember they extended over some weeks. I had been interested in automatic writing, and on attempting it found I could write with ease. Many messages came, ostensibly from various persons, but none really evidential. All were apparently friendly, and well-meaning in the usual rather high-flown style of such communications. Several were quite untrue.

"I might mention that the house in which these things occurred is very old, and although no regular haunting seems to have taken place, yet steps and knocks have been heard. I heard them myself, and one visitor claimed to have felt 'influences' while in the house.

"My husband was an invalid, and my two children were very young, so I had to go through the trouble alone. It began by the disappearance of a brooch. I thought I must have dropped it, but when I asked my little girl if she had seen it, a curious excited expression came across her face; she ran immediately to a chair and found it under a piece of material,which I had stretched over a worn place. Naturally one would think she had hidden it, but this she denied, and she was a very truthful child. The next day two brooches were gone, and she found them at once under the hall door-mat.

"From that out I had no peace. All my things—shoes, brushes, candles, ornaments, silver, teapots, clothes, books, work-box, pens, etc.—began to get lost, and were found in the most extraordinary places. My husband knew nothing of all this, as he was not well enough to be told. The children certainly had no hand in the matter, as these things happened just the same if they were out of the house, or away for the whole day. Articles were taken from locked cupboards and found sometimes in a drain outside the house, or up a tree. My little girl, if at home, was usually the finder; she used to get a queer excited look, and run to the place and bring back the article. Frequently she found things that I had *not* missed; she always thought that they were *like* things I had, but expected to be allowed to keep them.

"I never *saw* anything moving but the movement of articles used to take place very quickly at times. Whatever, or whoever, played these tricks certainly possessed very low intelligence, as the same hiding-places were used again and again. Favourite spots for concealment were under clothes in drawers, in clothes-baskets, and in shut window-seats. A frequently chosen place was

the grate; silver brushes and combs were placed in it and boots then piled up over them. Nothing was ever taken clean away, only hidden.

"I shall now relate to you in detail some instances of objects being taken and recovered. One morning I went into the children's room, which opened off an inside hall. They were not there, and I noticed a brush and comb on the mantelpiece, where I had been brushing my daughter's hair overnight by the fire. I was glad to see it had not been taken, and called to the maid to know where were the children. She replied that my little girl had taken her brother to get something on the avenue. We both stepped into the outside hall, and met the children running in with some parrot's feathers that had always been in the hall. My daughter said she had found them in a drain far down the avenue. I asked her how she knew that they were there; she looked puzzled, and said that she could not tell. The maid, who had been beside me all this time, returned to the kitchen, and I took the children to their room to finish their dressing. It was only a step away, and I had only been absent a minute, but during that time the brush and comb had been moved into the grate, from which I hurriedly withdrew them.

"My husband went out one morning, leaving on the dining-room mantelpiece two S-shaped hooks for tackling the cart, which he had sent for by post. He was away for the day. I noticed that the hooks were gone, but thought he had put them away before leaving. When he came back in the evening he missed them, and asked where they were. Then I knew! The children were in bed, but not asleep, so I hurried to their room and asked my daughter if she had seen two hooks that were on the dining-room mantelpiece. She at once sat up in bed, and that excited look I now knew so well came over her face. 'I didn't see them,' she said, 'but what were they like, and I'll guess!' I described them as best I could. 'Try in the dining-room arm-chair, at the side, put your hand far down!' I did so, and from the depths of the upholstering I drew up the hooks.

"Another day we were all sitting in the dining-room, where the fire was, when early dinner was brought in. I was seated by the fireside, and my work-box lay on a small table close to my elbow. The kitchen opened off the dining-room, the door being some distance away from the fireplace. We went over to the table and had dinner; the maid never went near the fire, and no one else left the room. After dinner my daughter, who was still at table talking to her brother, suddenly looked up, and said, 'Mother, I wonder where is your work-box!' I had not thought of it, but on looking towards the table saw that it had disappeared. I hunted about, then called my disappeared. I hunted about, then called my daughter, and asked her to look for it. She ran from the room, and in a few moments brought it back. I asked where it was. 'Under the window-seat in the drawing room.' I asked how she knew it was there—she could not tell! Late in the evening my brother-in-law (my sole confidant) came in. We were still by the dining-room fire. I was telling him of the latest happenings, and when I came to the work-box I pointed to the table where it was—and found that it was gone again! I called my daughter, gave her a small lamp, as the house was dark, and told her to carry it carefully and look for my work-box. She found it again in the drawing-room, but I think in a different corner.

"Nothing very large was ever moved; the largest object removed was a bolster, which was carried to my son's bed from my daughter's. Our maid scalded her foot on one occasion, and so never took an unnecessary step; I sent her home to recover, and got another in the middle of it all, but it made no difference. I spent my time trying to find things and put them back in their places before anyone could notice their absence.

"When these 'happenings' began to decrease I thought if I went away the spell might be broken; and though very reluctant to leave the children open to blame without being there to defend them, I went. I never missed as much as a pin while away; a few things were lost at home, but nothing very serious. After my return odd things disappeared, but at longer intervals.

"When I thought it all at an end a curious thing happened. I lost a pair of scissors suddenly, and after a couple of months found it inside the bottom hem of a tweed winter skirt. This had never been torn, or mended, all ripped. The sewing was so fine that I had a good deal of trouble in getting it out. That was the last thing that occurred in my home, but, a little later, when staying in a house where séances were held, a few of my clothes were taken during the night, and hidden at the far end of my bedroom.

"At the commencement of the troubles I asked the spirit correspondents what was the reason for these disturbances and strange happenings, and It (or They) said it was due to bad spirits who were trying to frighten me, and cause me to stop my automatic writing, which was helping me. Thereupon I determined to give it up altogether, so if that was their object they certainly succeeded in it!"

The following extraordinary personal experience is sent by a lady, well known to the present writer, but who requests that all names be omitted. Whatever explanation we may give of it, the good faith of the tale is beyond doubt.

"Two or three months after my father-in-law's death my husband, myself, and three small sons lived in the west of Ireland. As my husband was a young barrister, he had to be absent from home a good deal. My three boys slept in my bedroom, the eldest being about four, the youngest some months. A fire was kept up every night, and with a young child to look after, I was naturally awake more than once during the night. For many nights I believed I distinctly saw my father-in-law sitting by the fireside. This happened, not once or twice, but many times. He was passionately fond of his eldest grandson, who lay sleeping calmly in his cot. Being so much alone probably made me restless and uneasy, though I never felt *afraid*. I mentioned this strange thing to a friend who had known and liked my father-in-law, and she advised me to 'have his soul laid,' as she termed it. Though I was a Protestant and she was a Roman Catholic (as had also been my father-in-law), yet I fell in with her suggestion. She told me to give a coin to the next beggar that came to the house, telling him (or her) to pray for the rest of Mr. So-and-so's soul. A few days later a beggar-woman and her children came to the door, to whom I gave a coin and stated my desire. To my great surprise I learned from her manner that such requests were not unusual. Well, she went down on her knees on the steps, and prayed with apparent earnestness and devotion that his soul might find repose. Once again he appeared, and seemed to say to me, 'Why did you do that, E—? To come and sit here was the only comfort I had.' Never again did he appear, and strange to say, after a lapse of more than thirty years I have felt regret at my selfishness in interfering.

"After his death, as he lay in the house awaiting burial, and I was in a house some ten miles away, I thought that he came and told me that I would have a hard life, which turned out only too truly. I was then young, and full of life, with every hope of a prosperous future."

That children, as well as grown-up people, can have supernormal experiences has been proved more than once by the stories in this book. A clergyman of the Church of Ireland, who does not desire to have his name made public, has sent the following account of an experience that befell him about the year 1885, when he was between five and six years old.

"I was staying for the summer with my paternal grandmother and my aunt in a pretty little house in Westmeath. About eleven o'clock one morning my grandmother, who was working in the sitting-room, sent me upstairs to her bedroom to find some spools of thread for her. No sooner had I entered her room than I was amazed to see a strange elderly gentleman sitting at the head of her bed in an arm-chair which I did not remember ever having seen before. He remained without speaking, looking at me with a kind expression on his face. Notwithstanding that I felt very cold and very frightened, principally because he was, as I can only put it, *all grey*, his face, hands, and clothes being only different shades of that colour. The fear I felt made me turn and run down as quickly as I could to my grandmother, crying out, 'There is a strange man in your room, and he is all grey!' I refused to go back again, and after both my relatives had assured me that nobody could be there, my aunt went up herself to investigate; she returned in a few minutes, looking very white and strained, and told my grandmother that no one was there now, and thereupon sent me off to the hayfield. Later in the same day, as well as I remember, they both cross-questioned me regarding the stranger; I told them all I could about him, adding the detail that he had no beard.

"Many years after, I think about 1900, my grandmother having died in the meantime, I was talking to my aunt on the subject of family portraits, and said how sorry I was not to have had any photographs of my grandparents, as I had only seen a portrait of my mother's father, and one grandmother in the flesh. She looked at me in an odd way for a few moments, and then asked me if I remembered the occurrence I have related above. I replied that I did, and retold the story; after a pause she said, 'That was your father's father—my father—I saw him, too, that morning!' More than that she would not tell me, except that the arm-chair—his favourite chair—had been given away after his death!

"My paternal grandfather, whom I saw that morning in the room, died many years before I was born; no portrait of him was in existence. I did not even know that he was clean-shaven; I assumed, childlike, that both my grandfathers were alike, as they were cousins and had the same name; and the magnificence of my *maternal* grandfather's beard was almost proverbial in the part of the country in which he lived."

Of all the strange beliefs to be found in Ireland that in the Black Dog is the most widespread. There is hardly a parish in the country but could contribute some tale relative to this spectre, though the majority of these are short, and devoid of interest. There is said to be such a dog just outside the avenue gate of Donohill Rectory, but neither of the compilers have had the good luck to see it. It may be, as some hold, that this animal was originally a cloud or nature-myth; at all events, it has now descended to the level of an ordinary haunting. The most circumstantial story that we have met with relative to the Black Dog is that related as follows by a clergyman of the Church of Ireland, who requests us to refrain from publishing his name.

"In my childhood I lived in the country. My father, in addition to his professional duties, sometimes did a little farming in an amateurish sort of way. He did not keep a regular staff of labourers, and consequently when anything extra had to be done, such as hay-cutting or harvesting, he used to employ day-labourers to help with the work. At such times I used to enjoy being in the fields with the men, listening to their conversation. On one occasion I heard a labourer remark that he had once seen the devil! Of course I was interested and asked him to give me his experience. He said he was walking along a certain road, and when he came to a point where there was an entrance to a private place (the spot was well known to me), he saw a black dog sitting on the roadside. At the time he paid no attention to it, thinking it was an ordinary retriever, but after he had passed on about two or three hundred yards he found the dog was beside him, and then he noticed that its eyes were blood-red. He stooped down, and picked up some stones in order to frighten it away, but though he threw the stones at it they did not injure it, nor indeed did they seem to have any effect. Suddenly, after a few moments, the dog vanished from his sight.

"Such was the labourer's tale. After some years, during which time I had forgotten altogether about the man's story, some friends of my own bought the place at the entrance to which the apparition had been seen. When my friends went to reside there I was a constant visitor at their house. Soon after their arrival they began to be troubled by the appearance of a black dog. Though I never saw it myself, it appeared to many members of the family. The avenue leading to the house was a long one, and it was customary for the dog to appear and accompany people for the greater portion of the way. Such an effect had this on my friends that they soon gave up the house, and went to live elsewhere. This was a curious corroboration of the labourer's tale."

Since the foregoing narrative was written, a lady, who does not wish to disclose her identity, has sent the experience of herself and others with the Black Dog.

"When my sister and I were children we liked nothing better than going on a visit to an uncle in Co. Tyrone, who lived in a large farmhouse to which a considerable farm was attached. The first time I remember going there I must have been about ten years of age. I was put to sleep in a larger room at the end of a long passage. One night I had the most vivid and terrible nightmare—if it was a nightmare!—that I have ever had in my life. I remember it as clearly as if it had only happened last night. I thought I woke and saw a huge curly black dog standing in the room looking at me. Then he came over to the bed with his mouth open, and his great red tongue hanging out. He snuffed me, and licked my hands and face; after which I saw him no more. I was paralysed with fear, and lay under the clothes for a long time in an agony of terror, and nearly suffocated with heat.

"Fifteen years later I met my cousin, the son of the house, who had been abroad, and was now staying with my father. I happened to mention to him the nightmare I had had in his father's house in Tyrone, and described the room in which it had happened. To my astonishment he declared that he had had a similar experience in the same room. Furthermore, every time he slept in that room the same thing happened; but the only difference between his experience and mine was that with the black dog there appeared to him an old woman. He said he was not asleep when he saw them.

"About a week later his sister came to see me. Without saying anything about the black dog, I began to talk to her about her old home, and it soon transpired that she had had a similar experience in that room, except that the dog alone appeared to her. There is nothing to add, except that I do not think it possible to explain away these facts by a theory of coincidence."

As we have already stated in Chapter VII, a distinction must be drawn between the so called *Headless* Coach, which portends death, and the *Phantom* Coach, which appears to be a harmless sort of vehicle. With regard to the latter we give two tales below, the first of which was sent by a lady whose father was a clergyman, and a gold medallist of Trinity College, Dublin.

"Some years ago my family lived in Co. Down. Our house was some way out of a fair-sized manufacturing town, and had a short avenue which ended in a gravel sweep in front of the hall door. One winter's evening, when my father was returning from a sick call, a carriage going at a sharp pace passed him on the avenue. He hurried on, thinking it was some particular friends, but when he reached the door no carriage was to be seen, so he concluded it must have gone round to the stables. The servant who answered his ring said that no visitors had been there, and he, feeling certain that the girl had made some mistake, or that someone else had answered the door, came into the drawing-room to make further inquiries. No visitors had come, however, though those sitting in the drawing-room had also heard the carriage drive up.

"My father was most positive as to what he had seen, viz. a closed carriage with lamps lit; and let me say at once that he was a clergyman who was known throughout the whole of the north of Ireland as a most level-headed man, and yet to the day of his death he would insist that he met that carriage on our avenue.

"One day in July one of our servants was given leave to go home for the day, but was told she must return by a certain train. For some reason she did not come by it, but by a much later one, and rushed into the kitchen in a most penitent frame of mind. 'I am so sorry to be late,' she told the cook, 'especially as there were visitors. I suppose they stayed to supper, as they were so late going away, for I met the carriage on the avenue.' The cook thereupon told her that no one had been at the house, and hinted that she must have seen the ghost-carriage, a statement that alarmed her very much, as the story was well known in the town, and car-drivers used to whip up their horses as they passed our gate, while pedestrians refused to go at all except in numbers. We have often *heard* the carriage, but these are the only two occasions on which I can positively assert that it was *seen*."

The following personal experience of the phantom coach was given to the present writer by Mr. Matthias Fitzgerald, coachman to Miss Cooke, of Cappagh House, Co. Limerick. He stated that one moonlight night he was driving along the road from Askeaton to Limerick when he heard coming up behind him the roll of wheels, the clatter of horses' hoofs, and the jingling of the bits. He drew over to his own side to let this carriage pass, but nothing passed. He then looked back, but could see nothing, the road was perfectly bare and empty, though the sounds were perfectly audible. This continued for about a quarter of an hour or so, until he came to a cross-road, down one arm of which he had to turn. As he turned off he heard the phantom carriage dash by rapidly along the straight road. He stated that other persons had had similar experiences on the same road.

IX

LEGENDARY AND ANCESTRAL GHOSTS

W HATEVER explanations may be given of the various stories told in our previous chapters, the facts as stated therein are in almost every case vouched for on reliable authority. We now turn to stories of a different kind, most of which have no evidence of any value in support of the *facts*, but which have been handed down from generation to generation, and deserve our respect, if only for their antiquity. We make no apology for giving them here, for, in addition to the interesting reading they provide, they also serve a useful purpose as a contrast to authenticated ghost stories. The student of folklore will find parallels to some of them in the tales of other nations.

The late Lord Walter Fitzgerald contributed the the following: "Garrett oge" (or Gerald the younger) "Fitzgerald, 11th Earl of Kildare, died in London on the 16th November 1585; his body was brought back to Ireland and interred in St. Brigid's Cathedral, in Kildare. He was known as 'the Wizard Earl' on account of his practising the black art, whereby he was enabled to transform himself into other shapes, either bird or beast according to his choice; so notorious was his supernatural power that he became the terror of the countryside.

"His wife, the Countess, had long wished to see some proof

of his skill, and had frequently begged him to transform himself before her, but he had steadily refused to do so, as he said if he did and she became afraid, he would be taken from her, and she would never see him again. Still she persisted, and at last he said he would do as she wished on condition that she should first of all undergo three trials to test her courage; to this she willingly agreed. In the first trial the river Greese, which flows past the castle walls, at a sign from the Earl overflowed its banks and flooded the banqueting hall in which the Earl and Countess were sitting. She showed no sign of fear, and at the Earl's command the river receded to its normal course. At the second trial a huge eel-like monster appeared, which entered by one of the windows, crawled about among the furniture of the banqueting hall, and finally coiled itself round the body of the Countess. Still she showed no fear, and at a nod from the Earl the animal uncoiled itself and disappeared. In the third test an intimate friend of the Countess, long since dead, entered the room, and passing slowly by her went out at the other end. She showed not the slightest sign of fear, and the Earl felt satisfied that he could place his fate in her keeping, but he again warned her of his danger if she lost her presence of mind while he was in another shape. He then turned himself into a black bird, flew about the room, and perching on the Countess's shoulder commenced to sing. Suddenly a black cat appeared from under a chest, and made a spring at the bird; in an agony of fear for its safety the Countess threw up her arms to protect it and swooned away. When she came to she was alone, the bird and the cat had disappeared, and she never saw the Earl again."

It is said that he and his knights lie in an enchanted sleep, with their horses beside them, in a cave under the Rath on the hill of Mullaghmast, which stands, as the crow flies, five miles to the north of Kilkea Castle. Once in seven years they are allowed to issue forth; they gallop round the Curragh, thence across country to Kilkea Castle, where they re-enter the haunted wing, and then return to the Rath of Mullaghmast. The Earl is easily recognised as he is mounted on a white charger shod with silver shoes; when these shoes are worn out the enchantment will be broken, and he will issue forth, drive the foes of Ireland from the land, and reign for a seven times seven number of years over the vast estates of his ancestors.

Shortly before '98 he was seen on the Curragh by a blacksmith who was crossing it in an ass-cart from Athgarvan to Kildare. A fairy blast overtook him, and he had just time to say, "God speed ye Gentlemen" to the invisible "Good People," when he heard horses galloping up behind him; pulling to one side of the road he looked back and was terrified at seeing a troop of knights, fully armed, led by one on a white horse. The leader halted his men, and riding up to the blacksmith asked him to examine his shoes. Almost helpless from fear he stumbled out of the ass-cart and looked at each shoe, which was of silver, and then informed the knight that all the nails were sound. The knight thanked him, rejoined his troop, and galloped off. The blacksmith in a half-dazed state hastened on to Kildare, where he entered a public-house, ordered a noggin of whisky, and drank it neat. When he had thoroughly come to himself he told the men that were present what had happened to him on the Curragh; one old man who had listened to him said: "By the mortial! Man, ye are after seeing 'Gerod Earla.'" This fully explained the mystery. Gerod Earla, or Earl Gerald, is the name by which the Wizard Earl is known by the peasantry.

One other legend is told in connection with the Wizard Earl of a considerably later date. It is said that a farmer was returning from a fair in Athy late one evening in the direction of Ballintore, and when passing within view of the Rath of Mullaghmast he was astonished to see a bright light apparently issuing from it. Dismounting from his car he went to investigate. On approaching the Rath he noticed that the light was proceeding from a cave in which were sleeping several men in armour, with their horses beside them. He cautiously crept up to the entrance, and seeing that neither man nor beast stirred he grew bolder and entered the chamber; he then examined the saddlery on the horses, and the armour of the men, and plucking up courage began slowly to draw a sword from its sheath; as he did so the owner's head began to rise, and he heard a voice in Irish say, "Is the time yet come?" In terror the farmer, as he shoved the sword back, replied, "It is not, your Honour," and then fled from the place.

It is said that if the farmer had only completely unsheathed the sword the enchantment would have been broken, and the Earl would have come to his own again.

In 1642 Wallstown Castle, the seat of the Wall family, in County Cork, was burnt down by the Cromwellian troops, and Colonel Wall, the head of the family, was captured and imprisoned in Cork jail, where he died. One of the defenders during the siege was a man named Henry Bennett, who was killed while fighting. His ghost was often seen about the place for years after his death. His dress was of a light colour, and he wore a white hat, while in his hand he carried a pole, which he used to place across the road near the Castle to stop travellers; on a polite request to remove the pole he would withdraw it, and laugh heartily. A caretaker in the place named Philip Coughlan used frequently to be visited by this apparition. He came generally about supper time, and while Coughlan and his wife were seated at table he would shove the pole through the window; Coughlan would beg him to go away and not interfere with a poor hard-worked man; the pole would then be withdrawn, with a hearty laugh from the ghost.

In the Parish Church of Ardtrea, near Cookstown, is a marble monument and inscription in memory of Thomas Meredith, D.D., who had been a Fellow of Trinity College, Dublin, and for six years rector of the parish. He died, according to the words of the inscription, on 2nd May 1819, as a result of "a sudden and awful visitation." A local legend explains this "visitation," by stating that a ghost haunted the rectory, the visits of which had caused his family and servants to leave the house. The rector had tried to shoot it but failed; then he was told to use a silver bullet; he did so, and next morning was found dead at his hall-door while a hideous object like a devil made horrid noises out of any window the servant man approached. This man was advised by some Roman Catholic neighbours to get the priest, who would "lay" the thing. The priest arrived, and with the help of a jar of whisky the ghost became quite civil, till the last glass in the jar, which the priest was about to empty out for himself, whereupon the ghost or devil made himself as thin and long as a Lough Neagh eel, and slipped himself into the jar to get the last drops. But the priest put the cork into its place and hammered it in, and, making the sign of the Cross on it, he had the evil thing secured. It was buried in the cellar of the rectory, where on some nights it can still be heard calling to be let out.

A story of a phantom rat, which comes from Limerick, is only one of many which show the popular Irish belief in hauntings by various animals. Many years ago, the legend runs, a young man was making frantic and unacceptable love to a girl. At last, one day when he was following her in the street, she turned on him and, pointing to a rat which some boys had just killed, said, "I'd as soon marry that rat as you." He took her cruel words so much to heart that he pined away and died. After his death the girl was haunted at night by a rat, and in spite of the constant watch of her mother and sisters she was more than once bitten. The priest was called in and could do nothing, so she determined to emigrate. A coasting vessel was about to start for Queenstown, and her friends, collecting what money they could, managed to get her on board. The ship had just cast off from the quay, when shouts and screams were heard up the street. The crowd scattered, and a huge rat with fiery eyes galloped down to the quay. It sat upon the edge screaming hate, sprang off, and did not reappear. After that, we are told, the girl was never again haunted.

A legend of the Tirawley family relates how a former Lord Tirawley, who was a very wild and reckless man, was taken from this world. One evening, it is said, just as the nobleman was preparing for a night's carouse, a carriage drove up to his door, a stranger asked to see him and, after a long private conversation, drove away as mysteriously as he had come. Whatever words had passed they had a wonderful effect on the gay lord, for his ways were immediately changed, and he lived the life of a reformed man. As time went on the effect of whatever awful warning the mysterious visitor had given him wore off, and he began to live a life even more wild and reckless than before. On the anniversary of the visit he was anxious and gloomy, but he tried to make light of it. The day passed, and at night there was high revelry in the banqueting hall. Outside it was wet and stormy, when just before midnight the sound of wheels was heard in the courtyard. All the riot stopped; the servants opened the door in fear and trembling: outside stood a huge dark coach with four black horses. The "fearful guest" entered and beckoned to Lord Tirawley, who followed him to a room off the hall. The friends, sobered by fear, saw through the door the stranger drawing a ship on the wall; the piece of wall then detached itself and the ship grew solid, the stranger climbed into it, and Lord Tirawley followed without a struggle. The vessel then sailed away into the night, and neither it nor its occupants were ever seen again.

The above tale is a good example of how a legend will rise superior to the ordinary humdrum facts of life, for it strikes us at once that the gloomy spectre went to unnecessary trouble in constructing a ship, even though the task proved so simple to his gifted hands. But the coach was at the door, and surely it would have been less troublesome to have used it.

A strange legend is told of a house in the Boyne valley. It is said that the occupant of the guest chamber was always wakened on the first night of his visit, then he would see a pale light and the shadow of a skeleton "climbing the wall like a huge spider." It used to crawl out on to the ceiling, and when it reached the middle would materialise into apparent bones, holding on by its hands and feet; it would break in pieces, and first the skull and then the other bones would fall on the floor. One person had the courage to get up and try to seize a bone, but his hand passed through to the carpet though the heap was visible for a few seconds.

The following story can hardly be called *legendary*, though it may certainly be termed ancestral. The writer's name is not given, but he is described as a rector and Rural Dean in the late Established Church of Ireland, and a Justice of the Peace for two counties. It has this added interest that it was told to Queen Victoria by the Marchioness of Ely.

"Loftus Hall, in County Wexford, was built on the site of a stronghold erected by Raymond, one of Strongbow's followers. His descendants forfeited it in 1641, and the property subsequently fell into the hands of the Loftus family, one of whom built the house and other buildings. About the middle of the eighteenth century, there lived at Loftus Hall Charles Tottenham, a member of the Irish Parliament, known to fame as 'Tottenham and his Boots,' owing to his historic ride to the Irish capital in order to give the casting vote in a motion which saved £80,000 to the Irish Treasury.

"The second son, Charles Tottenham, had two daughters, Elizabeth and Anne, to the latter of whom our story relates. He came to live at Loftus Hall, the old baronial residence of the family, with his second wife and the two above-mentioned daughters of his first wife. Loftus Hall was an old rambling mansion, with no pretence to beauty: passages that led nowhere, large dreary rooms, small closets, various unnecessary nooks and corners, panelled or wainscotted walls, and a *tapestry chamber*. Here resided at the time my story commences Charles Tottenham, his second wife and his daughter Anne; Elizabeth, his second daughter, having been married. The father was a cold austere man; the stepmother such as that unamiable relation is generally represented to be. What and how great the state of lonely solitude and depression of mind of poor Anne must have been in such a place, without neighbours or any home sympathy, may easily be imagined.

"One wet and stormy night, as they sat in the large drawing-room, they were startled by a loud knocking at the outer gate, a most surprising and unusual occurrence. Presently the servant announced that a young gentleman on horseback was there requesting lodging and shelter. He had lost his way, his horse was knocked up, and he had been guided by the only light which he had seen. The stranger was admitted and refreshed, and proved himself to be an agreeable companion and a finished gentleman—far too agreeable for the lone scion of the House of Tottenham, for a sad and mournful tale follows, and one whose strange results continued almost to the present day.

"Much mystery has involved the story at the present point, and in truth the matter was left in such silence and obscurity, that, but for the acts of her who was the chief sufferer in it through several generations, nothing would now be known. The fact, I believe, was—which was not unnatural under the circumstances— that this lonely girl formed a strong attachment to this gallant youth chance had brought to her door, which was warmly returned. The father, as was his stern nature, was obdurate, and the wife no solace to her as she was a step-mother. It is only an instance of the refrain of the old ballad, 'He loved, and he rode away'; he had youth and friends, and stirring scenes, and soon forgot his passing attachment. Poor Anne's reason gave way.

"The fact is but too true, she became a confirmed maniac, and had to be confined for the rest of her life in the tapestried chamber before mentioned, and in which she died. A strange legend was at once invented to account for this calamity: it tells how the horseman proved such an agreeable acquisition that he was invited to remain some days, and made himself quite at home, and as they were now four in number whist was proposed in the evenings. The stranger, however, with Anne as his partner, invariably won every point; the old couple never had the smallest success. One night, when poor Anne was in great delight at winning so constantly, she dropped a ring on the floor, and, suddenly diving under the table to recover it, was terrified to see that her agreeable partner had an unmistakably cloven foot. Her screams made him aware of her discovery, and he at once vanished in a thunder-clap leaving a brimstone smell behind him. The poor girl never recovered from the shock, lapsed from one fit into another, and was carried to the tapestry room from which she never came forth alive.

"This story of his Satanic majesty got abroad, and many tales are told of how he continued to visit and disturb the house. The noises, the apparitions, and disturbances were innumerable, and greatly distressed old Charles Tottenham, his wife, and servants. It is said that they finally determined to call in the services of their parish priest, a Father Broders, who, armed with all the exorcisms of the Church, succeeded in confining the operations of the evil spirit to one room—the tapestry room.

"Here, then, we have traced from the date of the unhappy girl's misfortune that the house was disturbed by something supernatural, and that the family sought the aid of the parish priest to abate it, and further that the tapestry room was the scene of this visitation.

"But the matter was kept dark, all reference to poor Anne was avoided, and the belief was allowed to go abroad that it was Satan himself who disturbed the peace of the family. Her parents were ready to turn aside the keen edge of observation from her fate, preferring rather that it should be believed that they were haunted by the Devil, so that the story of her wrongs should sink into oblivion, and be classed as an old wives' tale of horns and hoofs. The harsh father and stepmother have long gone to the place appointed for all living. The Loftus branch of the family are in possession of the Hall. Yet poor Anne has kept her tapestried chamber by nearly the same means which compelled her parents to call in the aid of the parish priest so long ago.

"But to my tale: about the end of the last century my father was invited by Mrs. Tottenham to meet a large party at the Hall. He rode, as was then the custom in Ireland, with his pistols in his holsters. On arriving he found the house full, and Mrs. Tottenham apologised to him for being obliged to assign to him the tapestry chamber for the night, which, however, he gladly accepted, never having heard any of the stories connected with it.

"However, he had scarcely covered himself in the bed when suddenly something heavy leaped upon it, growling like a dog. The curtains were torn back, and the clothes stripped from the bed. Supposing that some of his companions were playing tricks, he called out that he would shoot them, and seizing a pistol he fired up the chimney, lest he should wound one of them. He then struck a light and searched the room diligently, but found no sign or mark of anyone, and the door locked as he had left it on retiring to rest. Next day he informed his hosts how he had been annoyed, but they could only say that they would not have put him in that room if they had had any other to offer him.

"Years passed on, when the Marquis of Ely went to the Hall to spend some time there. His valet was put to sleep in the tapestry chamber. In the middle of the night the whole family was aroused by his dreadful roars and screams, and he was found lying in another room in mortal terror. After some time he told them that, soon after he had lain himself down in bed, he was startled by the rattling of the curtains as they were torn back, and looking up he saw a tall lady by the bedside dressed in stiff brocaded silk; whereupon he rushed out of the room screaming with terror.

"Years afterwards I was brought by my father with the rest of the family to the Hall for the summer bathing. Attracted by the quaint look of the tapestry room, I at once chose it for my bedroom, being utterly ignorant of the stories connected with it. For some little time nothing out of the way happened. One night, however, I sat up much later than usual to finish an article in a magazine I was reading. The full moon was shining clearly in through two large windows, making all as clear as day. I was just about to get into bed, and, happening to glance towards the door, to my great surprise I saw it open quickly and noiselessly, and as quickly and noiselessly shut again, while the tall figure of a lady in a stiff dress passed slowly through the room to one of the curious closets already mentioned, which was in the opposite corner. I rubbed my eyes. Every possible explanation but the true one occurred to my mind, for the idea of a ghost did not for a moment enter my head. I quickly reasoned myself into a sound sleep and forgot the matter.

"The next night I again sat up late in my bedroom, preparing a gun and ammunition to go and shoot sea-birds early next morning, when the door again opened and shut in the same noiseless manner, and the same tall lady proceeded to cross the room quietly and deliberately as before towards the closet. I instantly rushed at her, and threw my right arm around her, exclaiming 'Ha! I have you now!' To my utter astonishment my arm passed through her and came with a thud against the bedpost, at which spot she then was. The figure quickened its pace, and as it passed the skirt of its dress lapped against the curtain and I marked distinctly the pattern of her gown—a stiff brocaded silk.

"The ghostly solution of the problem did not yet enter my mind. However, I told the story at breakfast next morning. My father, who had himself suffered from the lady's visit so long before, never said a word, and it passed as some folly of mine. So slight was the impression it made on me at the time that, though I slept many a night after in the room, I never thought of watching or looking out for anything.

"Years later I was again a guest at the Hall. The Marquis of Ely and his family, with a large retinue of servants, filled the house to overflowing. As I passed the housekeeper's room I heard the valet say: 'What! I to sleep in the tapestry chamber? Never! I will leave my lord's service before I sleep there!' At once my former experience in that room flashed upon my mind. I had never thought of it during the interval, and was still utterly ignorant of

Anne Tottenham; so when the housekeeper was gone I spoke to the valet and said, 'Tell me why you will not sleep in the tapestry room, as I have a particular reason for asking.' He said, 'Is it possible that you do not know that Miss Tottenham passes through that room every night, and, dressed in a stiff flowered silk dress, enters the closet in the corner?' I replied that I had never heard a word of her till now, but that I had, a few years before, twice seen a figure exactly like what he had described, and passed my arm through her body. 'Yes,' said he, 'that was Miss Tottenham, and, as is well known, she was confined—mad—in that room, and died there, and, they say, was buried in that closet.'

"Time wore on and another generation arose, another owner possessed the property—the grandson of my friend. In the year 185–, he being then a child came with his mother, the Marchioness of Ely, and his tutor, the Rev. Charles Dale, to the Hall for the bathing season. Mr. Dale was no imaginative person—a solid, steady, highly educated English clergyman, who had never even heard the name of Miss Tottenham. The tapestry room was his bed-chamber. One day in the late autumn of that year I received a letter from the uncle of the Marquis, saying, 'Do tell me what it was you saw long ago in the tapestry chamber, for something strange must have happened to the Rev. Charles Dale, as he came to breakfast quite mystified. Something very strange must have occurred, but he will not tell us, seems quite nervous, and, in short, is determined to give up his tutorship and return to England. Every year something mysterious has happened to any person who slept in that room, but they always kept it close. Mr. D—, a Wexford gentleman, slept there a short while ago. He had a splendid dressing-case, fitted with gold and silver articles, which he left carefully locked on his table at night; in the morning he found the whole of its contents scattered about the room.'

"Upon hearing this I determined to write to the Rev. Charles Dale, then Incumbent of a parish near Dover, telling him what had occurred to myself in the room, and that the evidence of supernatural appearances there were so strong and continued for several generations, that I was anxious to put them together, and I would consider it a great favour if he would tell me if anything had happened to him in the room, and of what nature. He then for the first time mentioned the matter, and from his letter now before me I make the following extracts:

"'For three weeks I experienced no inconvenience from the lady, but one night, just before we were about to leave, I had sat up very late. It was just one o'clock when I retired to my bedroom, a very beautiful moonlight night. I locked my door, and saw that the shutters were properly fastened, as I did every night. I had not lain myself down more than about five minutes before something jumped on the bed making a growling noise; the bed-clothes were pulled off though I strongly resisted the pull. I immediately sprang out of bed, lighted my candle, looked into the closet and under the bed, but saw nothing.'

"Mr. Dale goes on to say that he endeavoured to account for it in some such way as I had formerly done, having never up to that time heard one word of the lady and her doings in that room. He adds, 'I did not see the lady or hear any noise but the growling.'

"Here then is the written testimony of a beneficed English clergyman, occupying the responsible position of tutor to the young Marquis of Ely, a most sober-minded and unimpressionable man. He repeats in 1867 almost the very words of my father when detailing his experience in that room in 1790—a man of whose existence he had never been cognisant, and therefore utterly ignorant of Miss Tottenham's doings in that room nearly eighty years before.

"In the autumn of 1868 I was again in the locality, at Dunmore, on the opposite side of the Waterford Estuary. I went across to see the old place and what alterations Miss Tottenham had forced the proprietors to make in the tapestry chamber. I found that the closet into which the poor lady had always vanished was taken away, the room enlarged, and two additional windows put in: the old tapestry had gone and a billiard-table occupied the site of poor Anne's bed. I took the old housekeeper aside, and asked her to tell me how Miss Tottenham bore these changes in her apartment. She looked quite frightened and most anxious to avoid the question, but at length hurriedly replied, 'Oh, Master George! don't talk about her: last night she made a horrid noise knocking the billiard-balls about!'

"I have thus traced with strict accuracy this most real and true tale, from the days of 'Tottenham and his Boots' to those of his great-great-grandson. Loftus Hall has since been wholly rebuilt, but I have not heard whether poor Anne Tottenham has condescended to visit it, or is wholly banished at last."

X

MISTAKEN IDENTITY— CONCLUSION

WE have given various instances of ghostly phenomena wherein the witnesses have failed at first to realise that what they saw partook in any way of the abnormal. There are also many cases where a so-called ghost has turned out to be something very ordinary. Though more often than not such incidents are of a very trivial or self-explanatory nature (*e.g.* where a sheep in a churchyard almost paralysed a midnight wayfarer till he summoned up courage to investigate), there are many which have an interest of their own and which often throw into prominence the extraordinary superstitions and beliefs which exist in a country.

Our first story, which is sent us by Mr. De Lacy of Dublin, deals with an incident that occurred in the early part of last century. An epidemic which was then rife in the city was each day taking its toll of the unhappy citizens. The wife of a man living in Merrion Square was stricken down and hastily buried in a churchyard in Donnybrook which is now closed. On the night after the funeral one of the city police, or "Charlies" as they were then called, passed through the churchyard on his rounds. When nearing the centre he was alarmed to hear a sound coming from a grave close at hand, and turning, saw a white apparition sit up and address him. This was all he waited for;

with a shriek he dropped his lantern and staff and made off as fast as his legs would carry him. The apparition thereupon took up the lamp and staff, and walked to Merrion Square to the house of mourning, was admitted by the servants, and to the joy of the whole household was found to be the object of their grief returned, Alcestis-like, from the grave. It seems that the epidemic was so bad that the bodies of the victims were interred hastily and without much care: the unfortunate lady had really been in a state of coma or trance, and as the grave was lightly covered, when she came to she was able to force her way up, and seeing the "Charlie" passing, she called for assistance.

An occurrence which at first had all the appearance of partaking of the supernormal, and which was afterwards found to have a curious explanation, is related by Dean Ovenden of St. Patrick's Cathedral, Dublin. "At Dunluce Rectory, Co. Antrim," he writes, "I had a strange experience. There was a force-pump attached to the back wall of the house, and many people drew water from it, as it was better than any obtained at that time in Bushmills. We used to notice, when going to bed, the sound of someone working the pump. All the servants denied that they ever used the pump between 11 P.M. and 12 midnight. I often looked out of the back window when I heard the pump going, but could not see anyone. I tied threads to the handle, but although they were found unbroken in the morning the pumping continued, sometimes only for three or four moves of the handle. On many nights no pumping was heard. The man-servant sat up with a gun and the dog, but he neither saw nor heard anything. We gave it up as a bad job, and still the pumping went on. After about two years of this experience, I was one night alone in the house. It was a calm and frosty night and I went to bed about 11.30 P.M. and lay awake; suddenly the pump began to work with great clearness, and mechanically I counted the strokes: they were exactly twelve. I exclaimed, 'The dining room clock!' I sprang from bed and went down, and found that the clock was fast, as it showed two minutes past twelve o'clock. I set back the hands to 11.55 and lay in bed again, and soon the pumper began as usual. The explanation was that the vibration of the rising and falling hammer was carried up to the bedroom by the wall, but the sound of the bell was never heard. I found afterwards that the nights when there was no pumping were always windy."

The unbeliever will state that rats or mice are more often than not the cause of so-called ghostly noises in a house. That, at any rate, instances have happened where one or other of these rodents has given rise to fear and trepidation in the inmates of a house or bedroom is proved by the following story from a Dublin lady. She tells how she was awakened by a most mysterious noise for which she could give no explanation. Overcome by fear, she was quite unable to get out of bed, and lay awake the rest of the night. When light came she got up: there was a big bath in the room, and in it she found a mouse which had been drowned in its efforts to get out. So her haunting was caused by what we may perhaps call a ghost in the making.

The devil is very real to the average countryman in Ireland. He has given his name to many spots which for some reason or other have gained some ill-repute—the Devil's Elbow, a very nasty bit of road down in Kerry, is an instance in point. The following story shows how prevalent the idea is that the devil is an active agent in the affairs of this world.

A family living at Ardee, Co. Louth, were one night sitting reading in the parlour. The two maids were amusing themselves at some card game in the kitchen. Suddenly there was a great commotion and the two girls—both from the country—burst into the sitting-room, pale with fright, and almost speechless. When they had recovered a certain amount, they were asked what was the matter; the cook immediately exclaimed, "Oh, sir! The devil, the devil, he knocked three times at the window and frightened us dreadfully, and we had just time to throw the cards into the fire and run in here before he got us." One of the family, on hearing this, immediately went out to see what had caused all this trepidation, and found a swallow with a broken neck lying on the kitchen window-sill. The poor bird had evidently seen the light in the room, and in its efforts to get near it had broken its neck against the glass of the window.

An amusing account of a pseudo-haunting comes from County Tipperary, and shows how extraordinarily strong is the countryman's belief in supernatural phenomena. The incidents related occurred only a very short time ago. A farmer in the vicinity of Thurles died leaving behind him a young widow. The latter lived alone after her husband's death, and about three months after the funeral she was startled one night by loud knocking at the door. On opening the door she was shocked at seeing the outline of a man dressed in a shroud. In a solemn voice he asked her did she know who he was; on receiving a reply in the negative, he said that he was her late husband and that he wanted £10 to get into heaven. The terrified woman said she had not got the money, but promised to have it ready if he would call again the next night. The "apparition" agreed, then withdrew, and the distracted woman went to bed wondering how she was to raise the money. When morning came she did not take long in telling her friends of her experience, in the hope that they would be able to help her. Their advice, however, was that she should tell the police, and she did so. That night the "apparition" returned at the promised hour, and asked for his money. The amount was handed to him, and in a low sepulchral voice he said, "Now I leave this earth and go to heaven." Unfortunately, as he was leaving, a sergeant and a constable of the R. I. Constabulary stopped him, questioned him, and hauled him off to the barracks to spend the remainder of the night in the cell, where no doubt he decided that the haunting game has its trials.[17]

An account of a police-court trial which appeared in the *Irish Times* of 31st December 1913 emphasises in a very marked degree the extraordinary grip that superstition has over some of the country people. A young woman was on her trial for stealing £300 from the brother of her employer, Patrick McFaul of Armagh. District Inspector Lowndes, in opening the case for the Crown, told the bench that the money had been taken out of the bank by McFaul to buy a holding, for the purchase of which negotiations were going on. The money was carelessly thrown into a drawer in a bedroom, and left there till it would be wanted. A short time afterwards a fire broke out in the room, and a heap of ashes was all that was found in the drawer, though little else in the room besides a few clothes was injured. "The McFauls appeared to accept their loss with a complacency, which could only be accounted for by the idea they entertained that the money was destroyed through spiritual intervention—that there were ghosts in the question, and that the destruction of the money was to be taken as a warning directed against a matrimonial arrangement, into which Michael McFaul was about to enter." The accused girl was servant to the McFauls, who discharged her a few days after

---

[17] *Evening Telegraph* for Dec. 10, 1913.

the fire: but before this she had been into Derry and spent a night there; during her stay she tried to change three £20 notes with the help of a friend. But change was refused, and she had to abandon the attempt. "If some of the money was burned, some of it was certainly in existence three days later, to the amount of £60. One thing was manifest, and that was that an incredible amount of superstition appeared to prevail amongst families in that neighbourhood when the loss of such a sum as this could be attributed to anything but larceny, and it could for a moment be suggested that it was due to spiritual intervention to indicate that a certain course should be abandoned."

The foregoing tales have been inserted, not in order that they may throw ridicule on the rest of the book, but that they may act as a wholesome corrective. If *all* ghost stories could be subjected to such rigid examination it is probable that the mystery in many of them would be capable of equally simple solution—yet a remnant would be left.

And here, though it may seem somewhat belated, we must offer an apology for the use of the terms "ghost" and "ghost story." The book includes such different items as hauntings, death-warnings, visions, and hallucinations, some of which obviously can no more be attributed to discarnate spirits than can the present writer's power of guiding his pen along the lines of a page; whether others of these must be laid to the credit of such unseen influences is just the question. But in truth there was no other expression than "ghost stories" which we could have used, or which could have conveyed to our readers, within reasonable verbal limits, as they glanced at its cover, or at an advertisement of it, a general idea of the contents of this book. The day will certainly come when, before the steady advance of scientific investigation, and the consequent influencing of public opinion, the word "ghost" will be relegated to limbo, and its place taken by a number of expressions corresponding to the results obtained from the analysis of phenomena hitherto grouped under this collective title. That day is approaching. And so, though we have used the term throughout the pages of this book, it must not therefore be assumed that we necessarily believe in "ghosts," or that we are bound to the theory that all, or any, of the unusual happenings therein recorded are due to the action of visitants from the Otherworld.

We may now anticipate one or two possible points of criticism. It might be alleged that the publication of such a book as this would tend to show that the Irish nation was enslaved in superstition. Without stopping to review the question as to what should, or should not, be classed as "superstition," we would rejoin by gleefully pointing to a leading article in the *Irish Times* of Jan. 27, 1914, which gives a short account of a lecture by Mr. Lovett on the folklore of London. Folklore in London! In the metropolis of the stolid Englishman! The fact is that the Irish people are not one whit more superstitious than their cross-channel neighbours, while they are surely on a far higher level in this respect than many of the Continental nations. They *seem* to be more superstitious because (we speak without wishing to give any offence) the *popular* religion of the majority has incorporated certain elements which may be traced back to pre-Christian times; but that they *are* actually more superstitious we beg leave to doubt.

Another and more important series of objections is stated by one of our correspondents as follows. "I must confess that I can never reconcile with my conception of an All-Wise Creator the type of 'ghost' you are at present interested in; it seems to me incredible that the spirits of the departed should be permitted to return and indulge in the ghostly repertoire of jangling chains, gurgling, &c., apparently for the sole purpose of scaring housemaids and other timid or hysterical people." The first and most obvious remark on this is, that our correspondent has never read or heard a ghost story, save of the Christmas magazine type, else he would be aware that the above theatrical display is *not* an integral part of the "ghostly repertoire"; and also that persons, who are *not* housemaids, and who can *not* be classed as timid or hysterical, but who, on the other hand, are exceedingly sober-minded, courageous, and level-headed, have had experiences (and been frightened by them too!) which cannot be explained on ordinary grounds. But on the main point our correspondent is begging the question, or at least assuming as fully proved a conclusion which is very far from being so. Is he quite sure that the only explanation of these strange sights and weird noises is that they are brought about by the action of departed spirits (we naturally exclude cases of deliberate fraud, which in reality are very unusual)? And if so, what meaning would he put upon the word "spirits"? And even if it be granted that the phenomena are caused by the inhabitants of another world, why should it be impossible to accept such a theory, because of its apparent incompatibility with any conception of an All-Wise Creator, of whose workings we are so profoundly ignorant? Are there not many things in the material world which *to the limited human mind* of our correspondent must seem puzzling, meaningless, useless, and even harmful? He does not therefore condemn these offhand; he is content to suspend judgment, is he not? Why cannot he adopt the same attitude with respect to psychic phenomena? Our correspondent might here make the obvious retort that it is we who are begging the question, not he, because such happenings as are described in

MISTAKEN IDENTITY—CONCLUSION

this book have no existence apart from the imaginative or inventive faculties of certain persons. This would be equivalent to saying bluntly that a considerable number of people in Ireland are either liars or fools, or both. This point we shall deal with later on.

Our correspondent belongs to a type which knows nothing at all about psychical research, and is not aware that some of the cleverest scientists and deepest thinkers of the day have interested themselves in such problems. They have not found the answer to many of them—goodness knows if they ever will this side of the grave—but at least they have helped to broaden and deepen our knowledge of ourselves, our surroundings, and our God. They have revealed to us profundities in human personality hitherto unsuspected, they have suggested means of communication between mind and mind almost incredible, and (in the writer's opinion at least) these points have a very important bearing on our conceptions of the final state of mankind in the world to come, and so they are preparing the way for that finer and more ethical conception of God and His Creation which will be the heritage of generations yet unborn. The materialist's day is far spent, and its sun nears the horizon.

Another objection to the study of the subjects dealt with in this book is that we are designedly left in ignorance of the unseen world by a Wise Creator, and therefore that it is grossly presumptuous, not to say impious, on the part of man to make any attempt to probe into questions which he has not been intended to study. Which is equivalent to saying that it is impious to ride a bicycle, because man was obviously created a pedestrian. This might be true if we were confined within a self-contained world which had, and could have, no connection with anything external to itself. But the very essence of our existence here is that the material and spiritual worlds interpenetrate, or rather that our little planet forms part of a boundless universe teeming with life and intelligence, yet lying in the hollow of God's hand. He alone is "Supernatural," and therefore Transcendent and Unknowable; all things in the universe are "natural," though very often they are beyond our normal experience, and as such are legitimate objects for man's research. Surely the potential energy in the human intellect will not allow it to remain at its present stage, but will continually urge it onwards and upwards. What limits God in His Providence has seen fit to put upon us we cannot tell, for every moment the horizon is receding, and our outlook becoming larger, though some still find it difficult to bring their eyesight to the focus consequently required. The marvellous of today is the commonplace of tomorrow: "our notion of what is natural grows with our greater knowledge."

Throughout the pages of this book we have, in general, avoided offering explanations of, or theories to account for, the different stories. Here something may be said on this point. As we have already pointed out, the expression "ghost stories" covers a multitude of different phenomena. Many of these may be explained as "hallucinations," which does not imply that they are simply the effect of imagination and nothing more. "The mind receives the hallucination as if it came through the channels of sense, and accordingly externalises the impression, seeking its source in the world outside itself, whereas in all hallucinations the source is within the mind, and is not derived from an impression received through the recognised organ of sense."[18]

---

[18] Prof. Sir W. Barrett, *Psychical Research*, p111.

Many of these hallucinations are termed *veridical*, or truth-telling, because they coincide with real events occurring to another person. Illustrations of this will be found in Chapter VI, from which it would appear that a dying person (though the power is not necessarily confined to such) occasionally has the faculty of telepathically communicating with another; the latter receives the impression, and externalises it, and so "sees a ghost," to use the popular expression. Some hallucinations are *auditory*, *i.e.* sounds are heard which apparently do not correspond to any objective reality. Incomprehensible though it may appear, it may be possible for sounds, and very loud ones too, to be heard by one or more persons, the said sounds being purely hallucinatory, and not causing any disturbance in the atmosphere.

Some of the incidents may be explained as due to telepathy, that mysterious power by which mind can communicate with mind, though what telepathy is, or through what medium it is propagated, no one can tell as yet. Belief in this force is increasing, because, as Professor Sir W. Barrett remarks: "Hostility to a new idea arises largely from its being unrelated to existing knowledge," and, as telepathy seems to the ordinary person to be analogous to wireless telegraphy, it is therefore accepted, or at least not laughed at, though how far the analogy really holds good is not at all certain.

Again there is the question of haunted houses and places, to accounts of which the first five chapters of this book are devoted. The actual evidence for many of these may not come up to the rigorous standard set by the S.P.R., but it is beyond all doubt that persons who are neither fools, liars, nor drunkards firmly believe that they have seen and heard the things related in these chapters (not to speak of Chapters VI–VIII), or that they have been told such by those in whose statements they place implicit confidence; while so certain are they that they are telling the truth that they have not only written down the stories for the compilers, but have given their names and addresses as well, though not always for publication. Can we contemptuously fling aside such a weight of evidence as unworthy of even a cursory examination? This would hardly be a rational attitude to adopt. Various theories to account for these strange hauntings have been formulated, which may be found on pp. 199–200 of Sir William Barrett's *Psychical Research*, and so need not be given here.

Yet, when all is said and done, the very formulating of theories, so far from solving problems, only raises further and more complex ones, perhaps the greatest of which is, have the spirits of the departed anything to do with the matter? As we have shown, we hope with success, in the preceding paragraphs, many "ghosts" have no necessary connection with the denizens of the unseen world, but may be explained as being due to laws of nature which at present are very obscure. Does this hold good of all "ghosts," or are some of them to be placed to the credit of those who have passed beyond the veil, or perhaps to spirits, good or evil, which have never been incarnate? That is the problem for the future, for in the present state of our knowledge it would be premature to give a direct answer, either positive or negative.

This book was written with a twofold purpose: first, that of entertaining our readers, in which we trust we have been successful; secondly, to stimulate thought. For, strange though it may seem, authenticated "ghost stories" have a certain educative value. Taking them at their lowest they suggest inquiry into the strange workings of the human mind: at their highest how many strange lines of inquiry do they not suggest? For it is obvious that we have now arrived at one of those interesting periods in the history of human thought which might be described as the return of the pendulum. We are in the process of emerging from a very materialistic age, when men either refused to believe anything that was contrary to their normal experience, or else leavened their spiritual doctrines and beliefs with the leaven of materialism. The pendulum has swung to its highest point in this respect, and is now commencing to return, so perhaps the intellectual danger of the future will be that men, instead of believing too little, will believe too much. Now is the time for laying a careful foundation. Psychical research, spiritualism, and the like, are not ends in themselves, they are only means to an end. At the present state of thought, the transition from the old to the new, from the lower to the higher, it is inevitable that there must be confusion and doubt, and the earnest thinker must be prepared to suspend judgment on many points; but at a later stage, when all absurdity, error, and fraud, now so closely connected with psychical research in its various branches, will have been swept away, Truth will emerge and lift the human race to a purer and loftier conception of God and His universe.

NOTE ADDED IN PRESS

While these pages were passing through the press, a Rector in a southern diocese, who is known to the present writer, sent the following remarkable narrative, with the request of that all names be rigidly suppressed. The ladies who had these unpleasant experiences append a signed statement that the story is correct.

In 1877 the late Mr. G. came to reside at X., and made certain improvements in the original building. From time to time noises were heard in certain rooms in the old part of the house, footsteps, and sounds as if people were conversing. Sounds of footsteps were also heard on the gravel outside, and indeed at this particular time most of the noises occurred *outside* the house. Mr. G. frequently attempted to discover the cause of these, but in vain. During his lifetime, and for thirteen years afterwards, when his daughter Miss N. G. resided in the house, often alone, sounds such as the shutting of doors and the tramping of footsteps up and down the passages would be heard at intervals. But there would be long periods of six months or so when the no disturbance would be heard.

In 1916 there was a very marked recurrence of these sounds, especially at Easter and after. In 1920–22 these noises became very bad. A Miss M. A., who came to reside at X. in September 1920 with Miss G., and who had no previous knowledge of these disturbances, complained frequently of the opening and shutting of doors, knockings at the hall door and especially at bedroom doors, while she said she sometimes woke up in the night and felt as if some Presence of Evil were near her. Previous to this, visitors who had stayed in the house had, also complained of unpleasant noises in certain rooms.

In February 1922 the disturbances became more pronounced; there were knockings, opening and shutting of doors, and footsteps in the passages; while on two occasions a strange sound was heard as if a gust of wind swept violently up the passage—though outside the house there was no wind blowing. During this time there were no servants in the house, the only residents from October 1921 to March 1922 being Miss G. and Miss A., with a charwoman two nights a week.

In February Miss G. approached the Rector with a view to holding a service of exorcism in the house, which he did, on Wednesday, February the 22nd, at 9 A.M. The service took the form of certain prayers read from the services appointed in the

Priests' Prayer-Book for blessing a house, preceded by a celebration of Holy Communion. Special prayers were also used for protection from evil spirits, and for the repose of the souls of any persons associated with the house who might be in an unhappy condition. Since the holding of this service there has been no recurrence of these unpleasant noises and happenings, nor has there been perceived the strange consciousness of the presence of an evil personality, which had been felt by Miss G., Miss A., and others.

(Signed) A. B., Rector of C.

"We have read the foregoing, and declare that it is a true statement of the facts of the case.

"(Signed) N. G.

"M. A.

"10th of April 1922."

INDEX